Cedric Robinson

Between the Tides

The Perilous Beauty of Morecambe Bay

Cedric Robinson

The Queen's Guide to the Sands

GREAT NORTHERN

Cedric Robinson, Queen's Guide to the Sands

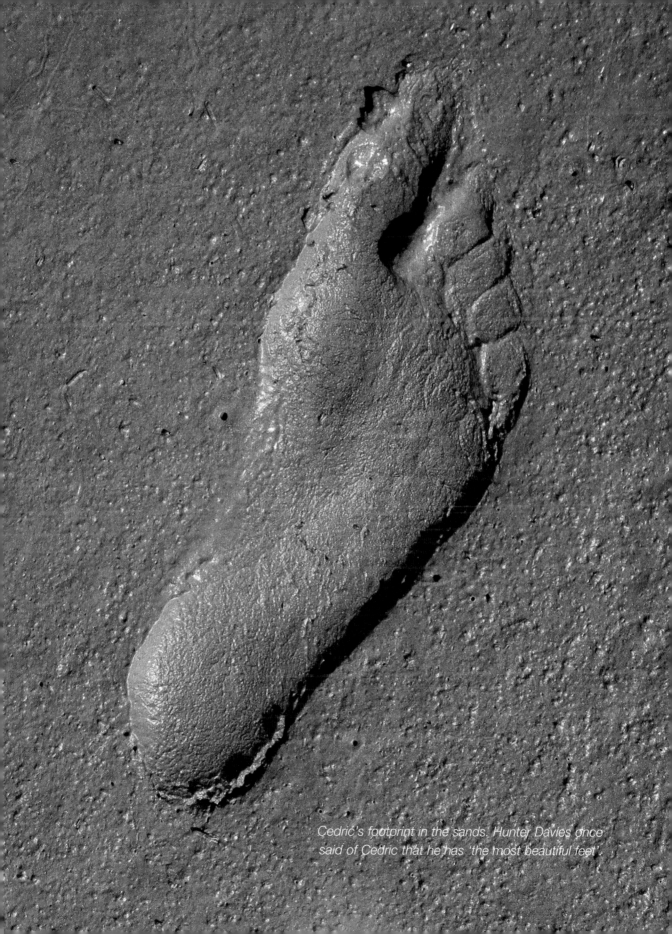

Cedric's footprint in the sands. Hunter Davies once said of Cedric that he has 'the most beautiful feet'.

Great Northern Books
PO Box 213, Ilkley, LS29 9WS
www.greatnorthernbooks.co.uk

ISBN: 978 1 905080 33 5

Design and layout: David Burrill

Printed in Spain

CIP Data
A catalogue for this book is available from the British Library

Acknowledgements

My typist Jane Keelan for making an excellent job of the typescript.

Susannah Bleakley – Morecambe Bay Partnership.

Jenny Kay, Morecambe Bay Task Group Democratic Support Officer,
Lancaster City Council.

My son Paul Nickson for the photographs and cover picture.
Uncredited photographs from the text are either by Paul or from my
own collection.

My wife Olive for reading through the script.

David Joy for giving me the opportunity to write once again about
Morecambe Bay.

Mike Carter.

Contents

H.R.H. The Duke of Edinburgh, seated next to Cedric Robinson, during the historic carriage crossing of the Sands on 30th May 1985. (photo: Tom Stephen)

Foreword

by H.R.H. The Duke of Edinburgh

WINDSOR CASTLE

Morecambe Bay is a very remarkable place. When the sands are exposed at low tide, it looks placid enough, and the same is true when they are covered by the sea – provided the weather is calm. What are not obvious to the naked eye are the quicksands, and the unwary can be taken by surprise by the speed at which the tide comes in.

Looking at the map, it appears that a route across the sands at low water would be a convenient short cut from Silverdale to Ulverston via Flookburgh. As this splendid book explains, the dangers of this route were already recognised in 1536 when the first King's Guide was appointed.

Cedric Robinson, the present Queen's Guide, has been guiding people across the Kent Sands for the last forty-five years, and he has some remarkable tales to tell. Back in 1985, I entrusted myself and my carriage and team of horses to his guidance across the sands, - and lived to tell the tale ! It was an extraordinary experience, particularly for an ex-sailor. Looking at the dramatic Lake District landscape round about, I kept feeling that I should have been in a boat.

I have no doubt that anyone interested in Britain's unique countryside, will find this a fascinating account of an unusual job in an unusual part of the country.

Philip

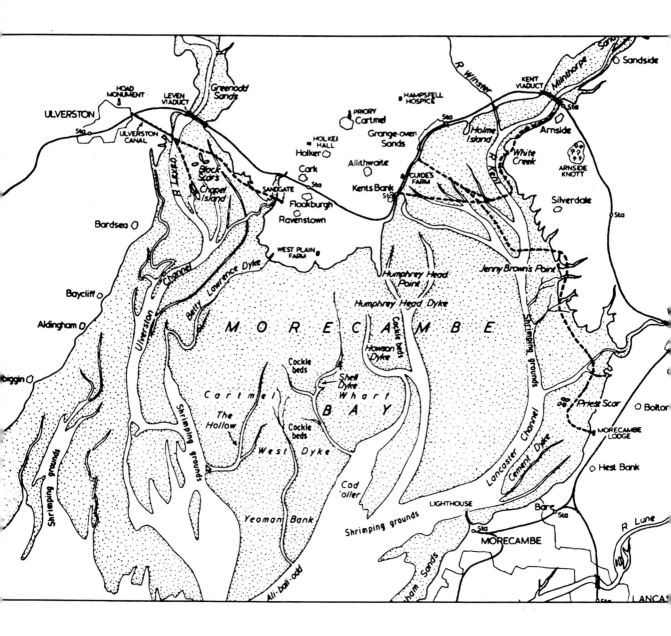

Morecambe Bay and its fishing grounds. The routes of the cross-Bay walks, shown by dotted lines, vary according to local conditions. (Original drawing by Olive Robinson).

Part 1
Across the Bay

The Morecambe Bay Walk

The Morecambe Bay Walk is probably now the best known and most popular of its kind in the country. The walks start in April and go through to October, or as long as the weather permits. Thousands of people come every year and sometimes there are as many as five hundred people on one walk. They come from all walks of life and think nothing of travelling great distances to take part in what I think, and I'm sure that they would agree, is an experience of a lifetime. A large number of these walks are organised to raise money for charities (the list gives an idea of how very popular they have become).

The organisers of each charity walk gather their supporters together and ask them to get sponsorship from their family and friends. Even the family dog can walk too, possibly with its own sponsorship. On the day of the walk they have an exciting and enjoyable time, walking the sands and raising money for their favourite charity. I think they must enjoy themselves as they come back year after year. Over the many years of crossing these famous sands, the amount raised for charity must have amounted to millions.

There are a lot of people who join a walk just for the sheer pleasure of doing it and being able to say that they have done it. What they have achieved certainly makes for a good topic of conversation in a social situation. In turn, it passes on the need for people to know, through their walk, the pleasures and the dangers and, most important of all, the environmental issues that are arising in our small part of the world.

Several times a year I have walks for children, who come from local schools, and these I enjoy enormously. Not only do the children love the walk, but they are very curious and want to know about everything that is happening. And, after all, they are our future and, hopefully, will remember what they have seen and learned, and when they are older will do what they can to preserve what we have.

The last walk of 2006 was organised for the whole of Sedbergh School to take part. Five hundred walkers raised over £20,000 towards the buildings of a children's hospice at Carlisle. It was quite a walk and the headmaster of the school sent us a very nice letter of thanks.

We even have a walk for little children. They come with their teacher and some helpers and I take them out on the Sandpiper, which is an open-sided trailer attached to my Leyland tractor. The little ones travel out into the Bay on the trailer and when we stop in a safe area they can have a run around. There are usually about thirty-plus of them and they absolutely love it.

A friend of mine, Larry Bennet from Grange, designed and built the Sandpiper for me to use on

Bay Walks for Charity

Charities taking part in walks across the Bay include:

Cumbrian Wildlife Trust

Macmillan Cancer Support

Blackpool & Fylde Leukaemia Research

Barnados

Galloways Society for the Blind

Christies for Cancer

RNLI Lifeboat Institution

Morecambe Bay Rescue

British Heart Foundation

Cystic Fibrosis Trust

British Red Cross

Keighley & District Association for the Blind

Arnside Landscape Trust

Arthritis & Rheumatism Council

Pendleside Hospice, Burnley

Bury Hospice

Derian House Children's Hospice

Manorlands – Bradford Hospice

Multiple Sclerosis Society

North West English Springer Spaniel Rescue

Morecambe Bay Partnership

National Children's Homes

Hope & Homes for Children

New Beginnings

Leeds Samaritans

Diabetes Association

St. Mary's Hospice, Ulverston

Chernobyl Children

Friends of the Lake District

Frances House Children's Hospice, Manchester

The Deaf Society

Blackpool Samaritans

El Shaddai Charitable Trust

Homes for Children, Cheshire

Coronary Care Appeal. Royal Lancaster Infirmary

The Meningitis Trust

Entrant number 535! Charity walks often attract large numbers, as in this instance where all the walkers were sponsored in aid of the British Heart Foundation. Cedric gives some firm words of advice.

the sands and give rides to the general public. This was at a time when funds were low and fishing in the Bay was very slack. Larry thought it would take off and people would be really interested in this new venture. It has seats the full length of the trailer and passengers sit back to back. It allows full views of the Bay when seated and has a roof over to keep off the rain. At first the Sandpiper was used to take people out on what I would call an educational visit. We would go out into the heart of the Bay and I would then stop the tractor for question and answer time. There was never a dull moment with everyone being so interested in what I had to tell them.

Sadly, I no longer make these kinds of trips with the Sandpiper because of the silting and the extensive areas of spartina grass out from Kents Bank covering the routes I used to take to Humphrey Head Point. We stopped to look for fossils on the rocks and admired the very old oak trees as well as the wildflowers and honeysuckle on the edge of the woods. The Sandpiper still has its uses as, apart from conveying young children, it also comes in very handy when taking film crews across the Bay to a location area. Its main role is as a back-up vehicle on all of my organised walks.

The eight mile walk starts just along from the pretty and picturesque promenade at Arnside in an area called Ash Meadow. There is a large sign pointing to the start of the walk opposite the Albion Hotel, where the road leaves the promenade and turns up a steep hill towards Silverdale. The walk takes about three hours to complete but can vary owing to the shifting channels and the meandering route that sometimes has to be followed.

If the weather is fine and clear, the panoramic views of the surrounding fells of Lakeland, Lancashire and Yorkshire can be astounding. Don't forget to bring along your camera so that you can take back a record of the day you crossed Morecambe Bay, which you can show to your friends and family, otherwise they may not believe you.

Guide's Farm, where I live with my wife Olive, is a very down-to-earth household. Although it is a Grade II listed building, to us it's a lovely old cottage full of warmth, character and charm. It couldn't be in a better position, as it sits facing Morecambe Bay to the west side of Grange-over-Sands.

At the bottom of the front garden is a lane that is a well used route for walkers. They come from Grange station, down the promenade, under the railway and, keeping the line to their left, they pass Guide's Farm and continue on to Kents Bank station. To the left of the cottage there is a level crossing that gives access over the railway and then leads to a slip road onto the Bay. To the back

Children and youngsters of all ages love the walk, as shown by these two splashing their way ahead of the crowd.

So too do dogs! These two are starting off firmly under control, but the temptation to cause trouble may prove irresistible.

The Sandpiper, an open-sided trailer attached to a Leyland tractor. Its main purpose now is to form a back-up vehicle on all organised walks.

and side of the house are four hedge-lined pastures, rising up and left towards Kents Bank, where we usually finish the Bay walks.

Olive is kept very busy dealing with enquiries for the walks. She seems to spend a big part of her day sitting with the phone in her hands and the diary on her lap, checking available dates and booking people in, sometimes from getting up in the morning to quite late at night. In between times we go out, and although we like to take your calls, we have to put the answerphone on and would prefer you to ring again later. Obviously, we cannot be by the phone all the time and it would be impossible to ring everyone back, as we get lots and lots of calls in the season. When you call again with your details, Olive will book you onto one of the walks with pleasure.

I recently received the following letter from a Yorkshire lady, who took part on one of my walks: "I knew before my husband and I came that we should enjoy the walk across Morecambe Bay, but having crossed with you on Saturday, September 16th, 2006, we found that it surpassed all our expectations. The weather was absolutely perfect, conditions underfoot were excellent, especially

Walkers gather at White Creek, Arnside, before moving out into the Bay.
(John Clegg)

Walkers leaving Arnside and heading towards the assembly point at Ash Meadow.

the warmth of the water, the scenery magnificent and the company fantastic – it really was a wonderful, unforgettable experience and a joy to meet you and to hear of all you had to tell us. The sight of so many children and happy dogs revelling in the water was one to remember forever. At Kents Bank we were pleased to meet your wife Olive too, an unexpected pleasure. I was delighted to find your beautifully written and illustrated book, which I have now read twice with enormous pleasure, and been amazed at the contents."

Later she wrote again to thank us both, for giving her and her husband the opportunity to walk across the Bay in safety and for all I do as the Queen's Guide. She very kindly added: "Long may you both continue to keep up the good work, and long may you both keep in good health." Olive and I much appreciated her words and were greatly touched. We look forward to meeting her and her family on a future crossing.

People often ask me if and when I am going to retire. I have to say, even though I am 74 years old, the thought has never crossed my mind. After all, my father lived to the ripe old age of 102 so I think I've got a few years left in me yet! Morecambe Bay is my life. I was born and bred to it and I still look forward to going out there each day, whether it be to my fishing nets or leading a walk across the sands and sharing my experiences and knowledge with the many people who join in.

I am also very lucky to have friends with me and they are a tremendous help. As I always 'lead from the front' as they say, I travel to Arnside with 'Whistler' John, who has been coming with me for many years. By blowing his whistle he brings everyone together. He makes sure that people don't wander off because they could soon get into trouble if they don't cross the river at the points we have marked out the previous day with 'brobs'. These are branches, which are gathered from our farm and are worked down well into the sand so that they will hold against the tides. They act as safety markers for the route of the walk.

John Barber, a Grange man, drives the Sandpiper out from Kents Bank and waits for us near the river. At this point some walkers feel the need for a rest and they can climb aboard whilst John drives them behind the main body of the walk. Two 'soft city boys', as John calls them, have joined the team. They are Barry and Ginger John, and they ride on the trailer, giving help where it is needed. They have had to learn about the Bay and the terminology that comes second nature to John and I. Gullets, gillamers, melgraves and sugary are but a few of the words that they now use freely. Mike, from the next village of Allithwaite, missed out on the walks during 2006 owing to an operation on his leg, but he is keen to be back with us and out onto the sands again.

The day before the big walks on Saturdays and Sundays we go out onto the Bay to test the safety of the sands. This is very important. My pals and I set off in my tractor and drive to Kents Bank station. It's Barry's job to ring the signal box, and there are three of them, Arnside, Grange and Ulverston, to check that we are allowed to cross over the railway line. Then we are off, down the tracks onto the sands and across the Bay to the river Kent. It takes us about an hour to get there.

I can read the sands as I go along, almost like you would read the morning paper. The safe areas, the not so safe and the areas to be definitely avoided. The bed of the river has to be tested on foot, so as we approach I bring the tractor to a halt within a safe distance and down we jump. Off with our wellies, we roll up our jeans well above the knee. We now each need a stick from the tractor. We use a longish ash or hazel stick to prod for quicksands when entering and wading through the river. At first glance it sometimes looks like the perfect crossing but, until we have entered and spread out, walking slowly and testing as we go, I cannot say what is under that stretch of water like I can on the sandbanks, so this has to be done thoroughly with nothing left to chance. It is not always a straightforward procedure and we've had many disappointments following high tides and heavy rainfall, or a combination of both. Sudden changes occur, making a relatively safe area into a dangerous environment in a short space of time.

Olive Robinson, who is kept busy on the phone dealing with enquiries for the walks.

Walkers set out past the 'brobs' – branches pushed well down into sand to mark the route of the crossing.

The summer of 2006 was one of the best seasons I have ever known for the cross-Bay walks. We had one of the driest of summers, but when the rains came down they came with a vengeance. They were extremely heavy and prolonged and on some occasions the entire riverbed moved, sometimes a quarter of a mile and, on occasion, even half a mile. It was almost unrecognisable from only a few days beforehand, with huge 'bracks', which are breakaways of sand, and the river running so fast and dangerous.

It can become a totally different environment in just a few days. When this happens there is just no way a walk can take place from one side of the Bay to the other. On these occasions the River Kent has to be well and truly avoided. But rather than disappoint the hundreds of people and their organisers, who have gone to all the trouble of getting themselves sponsored and have looked forward to the day out, a much safer walk can still take place. We then start from Kents Bank station and large stretches of water can still be crossed. The only thing we can't do is cross the River Kent. These walks can be just as interesting and fulfilling, and we then walk back to Kents Bank.

How it all Began

As one of a fishing family, I started following the sands of Morecambe Bay with my dad while still at school in Flookburgh. They must have been in my blood, as my father, grandfather and even my grandmother all worked the sands for their livelihood. I could only go in school holidays and at weekends.

As time moved on Flookburgh became a different village to the one I knew as a lad. One thing that stands out in my mind about those earlier days is the way the villagers spoke to one another – always in the local dialect. Going to school was a sore point for me because I did not enjoy it one little bit, but I must have done something right because I believe I was quite a good scholar. However, the call of the sands was never far away from my thoughts.

Flookburgh had a small community of people from all walks of life and the fishing families probably numbered around twenty or so. The fisherfolk were never closely knit, as most families over the years seemed to have their grievances regarding the sands. Yet our own family was very close, with my two sisters Peggy and Jean, my parents, one terrier dog called 'Crackers' and a cat which I had for twenty years.

A really big blow hit us when my father received his calling-up papers for World War Two. This took him away from us for five years and I often wonder how my mother managed. There was no running water or electricity in the house where we lived and I was born at No. 4 Market Cross, in a row of six cottages opposite the public house called 'The Hope and Anchor'.

The war had started and my sisters and I were still attending school. The village had a new policeman. The previous one was well liked by the local community but all the villagers feared this younger one. Every household had to black out the windows so that no flicker of light could be seen. This policeman was nicknamed 'Blackout Joe' by the villagers because he was always on the prowl. Woe betide those found without proper blackout - he was onto them like a ton of bricks.

He frightened the life out of my mother one day as she saw him coming to the front door of the cottage. Unfortunately, we were so poor that mother could not afford to renew our dog licence so, before opening the door to him, she told me to take our terrier dog quickly out of the back door, thinking he would not know about it. Too late! He immediately said to mother that we had a dog with no licence and we would have to pay a fine. 'Blackout Joe' was a heartless soul because to pay the fine mother had to take in washing. As we had no electricity, the water had to be heated on the open fire and the dolly tub and posser used. These hard times always remain in your memories but we managed because we had such good neighbours who were kind and friendly.

After five long years dad returned from the Army safe and sound, so we were able to start fishing in the Bay for a living once again. I just loved going onto the sands and felt that I never wanted to leave them, but at the age of eighteen I was called up into the Army for two years' National Service. Apart from visiting Morecambe and Blackpool, I had never been away from the village before, but now I had to report to Blandford in Dorset where I did my training. That was where, along with others, I was made to feel about two feet tall or should I say small! We were bawled at from dawn till dusk and could not do right for doing wrong. I am sure everyone in our squad did his best but it was not good enough. If you failed to salute an officer - and there were many of them - you were bawled at again. So, to get it right we would salute anything that moved, sometimes getting it wrong and made to feel such an idiot.

It did become more tolerable when the weeks of training were finally over and I was posted to a much smaller army camp at Sedgefield in County Durham. After twelve months I was moved to Fulwood Barracks at Preston where I was able to travel home at weekends now and again. I could then visit the local dances, which I always enjoyed. They were held at the Rink in Barrow-in-Furness, the Coronation Hall at Ulverston, or the Pier, the Winter Gardens or the Floral Hall in Morecambe. I was called upon to do fishing out in the Bay many times in the early hours after these enjoyable late nights out with my mates. But I could not wait for those two very long years to end and get back to my family and friends.

In spring 1960 I met Olive, who was a widow with four young children. Bill was the eldest aged thirteen years, then Robert, Diane and Paul. I asked Bill if he would like to earn some money by coming to help me with the market gardening as we had two smallholdings. He was a very good and willing help, gathering vegetables and packing them into the van ready for an early start to the market at Barrow-in-Furness on Wednesdays, Fridays and Saturdays, mum and dad had a stall there where they would sell our home-grown vegetables and also the flukes, shrimps and cockles caught out in the Bay by Bill and me.

This was the beginning of a lasting friendship with Olive and her family as we came to know each other very well. We married at St John the Baptist Church in Flookburgh on October 30th, 1961. I then moved into the house in Ravenstown where Olive had lived with her family. On 3rd January 1963 our daughter Jean was born and this added to our happiness.

Bill came out onto the sands with me regularly now that he had left school. One day, while out cockling miles from the shore, the North Western Sea Fisheries Officer, Gren Harrison, appeared as if from nowhere. He was the law officer of the sands and occasionally he would turn up and inspect the size of the cockles we were gathering. A well-built chap and very strong, he always wore a uniform similar to that of a naval officer and thigh boots that must have been a drag when walking all that way across the sands. I always thought him to be very fair with the local fishermen, as some of them did not always tow the line - and I always seemed to get on well with him.

On this occasion Bill and I were about to make ready for home when he offered to help load the cockles onto the cart. The bags weighed all of a hundredweight but he loaded all the cockles by himself without even taking down the cart's tailboard (known locally as the 'cart eck1). He just simply lifted them clean over and into the bottom of the cart without any effort at all. As we moved away from the cockle grounds making for home, Gren walked alongside the horse and cart chatting away. Then he happened to mention that the Guide over the sands at Grange, Mr Burrow, was retiring and he thought I would be a likely candidate for the job.

Gren talked freely about it and said that if I was at all interested I would have to apply in writing and he would give me the address. When Bill and I got home from the sands, the cockles were unloaded and the horse put in the stable down Moor Lane with a feed and off home we went. Olive had a meal ready for us, as out there on the sands always seemed to give us a good appetite. I told her what Gren had said about the Guide's job becoming available at Grange. She was quite happy living in Ravenstown but would go along with whatever I should decide. I applied in writing and was asked to go for an interview before finally being chosen as the 'Queen's Guide to the Kent Sands of Morecambe Bay' later in 1963.

In the meantime Olive's parents had come from Leeds to stay with us for a week's holiday. Her mother asked where were we going to live. Olive had never been to Cart Lane before so her mother suggested that they went along just to have a look at the place. They set off from Ravenstown and walked to Flookburgh Square with baby Jean in the pushchair. As they waited at the bus stop along came the bus for Grange. They took their seats not knowing where to get off, so the conductor put them off at Cardrona and kindly gave them directions to Cart Lane. Olive did not want to appear nosy as that is not her nature, but thought it would be nice to see the place and show her mother where we would be living.

Carter Road was downhill so Olive kept a tight hold of the pushchair with baby Jean strapped safely inside. This was a good precaution as this is a steep hill of about 1 in 4. They could see buildings at the lower end of the fields, close to the railway line so, at the bottom of Carter Road near the railway cottage and crossings, they turned right and within a short distance came across the house - Guide's Farm. There was a man standing just outside the front door. It was the Guide, Mr Burrow, but Olive had not met him before so she asked, "Please can you tell me if this is Guide's Farm?" and he replied "Yes" quite cheerfully. He said that he was Mr. Burrow and asked if Olive was my wife. "My missis is down Grange doing a bit of shopping so I can't show you round. We're not quite ready for moving as we've some apples to pick up in yon orchard" - which he pointed out. "And that's about it," he said.

We eventually moved to Guide's Farm, Grange, in early October 1963 and that is how it all began.

The First Walks

After settling into our new home, we were kept very busy during the winter months decorating and painting as well as going out onto the sands cockling. That winter was an extremely cold one and we did not have any heating that was adequate - no electricity, just the coal fire in an open grate in the large living room, When we got up in the morning the flannel in the bathroom was sometimes frozen to the sink. That does not happen any more because we now have calor gas heaters but still no central heating. If you are brought up to live without these kind of things when you are young, I am sure you become hardier and can put up with conditions that a younger generation would probably not tolerate today.

As soon as spring came along the first walk took place in April 1964. Guide's Farm had no telephone when we moved in so we had to rely on letters coming from interested parties. I had already received confirmation of whom I was to lead across the Bay. There were thirteen paratroopers on a military exercise on a day that weatherwise could not have been worse. Bitterly cold and heavy showers were the menu for the day, so my son Bill and I decided to wear our fishing gear and that meant oilskins and waders.

The crossing was from Hest Bank near Morecambe to Grange-over-Sands, which was a distance of about nine miles. The River Keer, which runs out into the Bay from Carnforth, is much smaller than the Kent but can be difficult to cross, especially if there has previously been heavy

The first walk of the 1964 season was also the first to be led by Cedric following his appointment as 'Queen's Guide to the Kent Sands of Morecambe Bay' in November 1963. Then only 30, he is seen on the right of the photograph.

rainfall. Luckily, we did not encounter any problems and walked on without looking back. We now set our line of journey for Jenny Brown's Point and, in the distance beyond, was the village of Silverdale. We made good time and being a small group of fit young men did not have to make any stops. Before long, the wide River Kent could be seen in the distance. As we approached you would have thought that in no way could we wade through the huge expanse of moving water but we did! A wide river is a much better and safer crossing than a narrow one.

With the fast flow our small party kept close together until the point where it began to get shallower, then the pace quickened. We crossed safely through the river onto the Grange shore.

The worst part of this crossing was the last hundred yards or so coming up the muddy shore near the bathing pool on the promenade, where we could hardly lift our feet from the suction of the sand. The officer in charge of the platoon said that the conditions on the day were ideal for his soldiers to have experienced, but this was one experience Bill and I wanted to forget!

The next walk - again from Hest Bank to Grange-over-Sands - took place in the middle of May and the weather had really warmed up for this one. It was a perfect day. I had travelled around to the other side by train from Kents Bank station to Carnforth, from where I managed to catch a bus to Hest Bank without much of a wait. This group comprised about twenty men and women ramblers.

The day was bright and visibility clear and Olive had seen us coming away in the distance through my powerful binoculars. She is very thoughtful and caring and had prepared a nice tea for us. Olive asked our daughter Diane to come to the crossing gates at Cart Lane with the message that she was expecting us to go along to the farm. We all trudged along the lane, Olive greeting us at the door with a smile and inviting everyone inside for tea. After taking off our shoes and leaving them and our haversacks in a tidy heap on the floor, we filed in and almost filled the living and sitting rooms. Olive had already made the sandwiches so she told us she would only be a minute brewing the tea.

Several of the walkers were by now desperate for the toilet so that took a bit of time, but then we all managed to find a seat somewhere to sit down and relax. All was quiet at first but then one after another they started to ask questions that were mainly about the old house and its history. Tea was brewed and Diane came round with the sandwiches, and then Olive appeared from the kitchen carrying one of those very large aluminium teapots. You will probably have seen them some time as they were used at wedding receptions, village hall parties, Women's Institute meetings and even at funerals. They are very heavy when full and have a handle at each side so that you can hold them steady and pour without spilling.

On this occasion our teapot came in very handy with these thirsty walkers and we had a really good time. They thanked us over and over again for our hospitality. Olive thought that this was the normal thing to do but, as time went on, the numbers of enquiries grew and grew into hundreds and more hundreds so now there is no way I could invite the walkers back to Guide's Farm for tea!

I never knew how Olive came to have that large aluminium teapot, but I do remember that our good neighbours in Cart Lane used to come and borrow it when they were having a family party or some other special occasion. One of our neighbours sadly borrowed it when her husband died. Olive and I were invited back to the house after the funeral along with the old teapot, which we still have.

I jotted down details of another walk in the 1960s in a notebook: "A nasty wet day, party left Hest Bank near Morecambe at 1.45 pm. The first obstacle was the River Keer. Found this very soft with the heavy rainfall, and was difficult to ford. Stopped the group halfway across the Bay on a high sandbank about two miles out from the village of Silverdale. After twenty minutes we set off for Grange crossing the River Kent between Blackstone Point and Holme Island, that being the only suitable place to cross. The river knee deep and a good crossing. We came ashore at the bathing pool at Grange-over-Sands on the promenade. Party consisted of twenty six from Blackburn Technical College, forty from Ripon in Yorkshire, others from Wakefield, Lancaster and Preston. One hundred and fifty walkers in all, and this was the first walk of the season."

Heading across the Bay on one of the early walks about 1964, with a much younger Cedric and Olive at the front. The striking feature of these early walks is the small numbers compared with the present day.

The walk, once an annual event, was now about to change. I would soon be organising about twelve walks a year and they seemed to catch on in a big way. A shorter working week was attributed to more walks taking place. People could arrange to come on either a Saturday or a Sunday and this was how it started to grow. The greater demand meant a lot of organisation for me to arrange each walk - the date, time, place to start and to finish, and checking each crossing beforehand.

High tide weekends are unsuitable so I have to plan for the neaps. Each season varies with the number of dates I can choose for a walk, but with the demand being as great as it is, I am now able to choose around thirty possible weekend dates and also a number of midweek ones. We are now encountering climate changes with milder winters and much milder and warmer springs. With these changes I find I can now organise and start the walks in April and continue right through the summer until the end of September. The Tourist Board Information Centre is now taking a wide interest with many enquiries regarding the dates and times of the walks and the public are travelling very long distances to take part in them.

Today, walking is a national hobby that is encouraged to help people keep fitter, healthier and live longer. The Morecambe Bay Walk fits that bill because people of all age groups and from all walks of life can take part and really enjoy the same experience - 'getting away from it all'! There are not many places in the world today where you can leave it all behind but Morecambe Bay with its peace and tranquillity is one of them.

The walk is now known internationally and enquiries come from afar. Whatever the weather on the day, people still genuinely enjoy the 'walk with a difference'. Although some of them are tired at the end, it is so rewarding that they always say how much they have enjoyed this unique and wonderful experience and ask to come again.

A Typical Crossing

For almost twenty-five years I led the walks from Hest Bank and Morecambe Lodge Farm across the sands to Grange. Looking back at photographs and cine film, it was rare to find many children or senior citizens included in the groups making the crossing. The railway station at Hest Bank was closed so many of the walkers would arrange to travel to the start by coach. Only a few went by train to Carnforth, where it was sheer luck if you could find a bus connection to take you the rest of the journey to Hest Bank. I preferred to walk rather than wait for a bus, not knowing whether one would turn up or not, so I was walking the whole time.

In those first years following my appointment the walks were hardly known compared with today, so it was rare to have someone from afar. Now it is quite different, as they are known both nationally and internationally, and also through the Internet. People travel long distances - and even all the way from America - just to take part in one or more of my walks.

Enquiries for this walk are now much reduced, as the alternative crossing from Arnside - the 'people's choice' - is the same distance and is also more exciting and suitable for all age groups. I still organise a few crossings from Hest Bank and Morecambe Lodge Farm. When I arrive to lead

The cross-Bay walk is generally a memorable and enjoyable experience (top left), especially if weather conditions are warm and sunny (bottom left). But on occasions storms can threaten (top right), or rain can reach deluge proportions (bottom right).

them, I am generally met with a motley crowd of all ages from seven to seventy. Almost everyone is carrying a rucksack and many of them are barefooted. It is almost a biblical scene as we set out across the sands - I carry my staff in my hand, whistle around my neck and my trainers stuffed into my rucksack. Moses must have been grateful when the Red Sea divided for them to cross.

We are about to cross an expanse of sand and water measuring one hundred and twenty square miles and some of the walkers are no doubt wondering how will I manage to keep track of them all in this vast wilderness. The first mile or so of the eight mile crossing is a process of acclimatisation or, in other words, getting used to the idea.

On these low tide weekends the ridges of sand plus the worm casts (and at these early stages there are millions of them) are hard on the feet if there is a warm dry spell. Youngsters on the walk seem to think that they are live worms on the surface and watch very carefully where they are putting their feet until I tell them differently!

Slowly, the group strings out to a length of about quarter of a mile. Ahead, the sands drop lower as we approach a shallow water crossing that feels warm underfoot, almost like warm water from the tap. This is what the youngsters in the group have been waiting for and, after asking permission to run on ahead, they race away and splash through the shallow water enjoying themselves to the full.

Now, as the walkers stride out they must feel the sense of freedom and adventure all in one. What else do they see out there? Well, there is beauty all around and ahead of us. In the distance are the Lake District fells and over to the right in the east are the far-off hills of Yorkshire and the flat-topped mountain of Ingleborough, Over to our left the West Coast runs down from Ulverston to Barrow and the islands of Furness. A square black blob on the horizon is the remains of the ancient Piel Castle off Walney Island and nearby Roa Island is where the Barrow lifeboat is launched into Morecambe Bay. Dotted on the northern shoreline is the pretty hometown of Grange-over-Sands.

Our first river crossing is the Keer, running out into the Bay from Carnforth and, although this is shallow during a dry spell, it is prone to quicksands after heavy rain. I spread the group at the edge of the river and ask them to wait while I go on ahead to ensure that all is well. Satisfied with conditions, I blow my whistle for the group to follow and give them a wave beckoning them towards me. Splash, splash, splash! - the youngsters race towards me ahead of the rest of the group and are having the time of their lives. Up on much higher ground clear from the water's edge, I stop and wait for everyone to leave the river before moving on.

The views from this point on a clear day are absolutely outstanding. This is the moment when the group can stand and take in the breathtaking beauty of the Bay all around. Looking back we can see Hest Bank, Morecambe and Heysham, and beyond is the Lune Valley. The River Lune winds its way down through Lancaster and enters the Bay below Middleton Sands.

Ashton Memorial with its dome-shaped head towers majestically above Williamson Park, Lancaster. Dubbed the 'Taj Mahal of the North', it was commissioned by Lancaster-born millionaire Lord Ashton for his family. From the upstairs gallery is one of the best views in the area with the Lakeland fells, the Isle of Man and Blackpool visible on a clear day.

Way ahead, to the left of Kents Bank and near to Allithwaite and Flookburgh, is Humphrey Head, the limestone headland called 'Boxhill of the North' because of its wide variety of flora. Jutting out into the Bay, the headland is about sixty feet above sea level at its highest point. Local folk have always called it Humphrey Head Point and it was famous in the early twentieth century when people

A welcome stop at the halfway stage of the walk in the heart of Morecambe Bay.

came along and drank from the famous 'holy well' of St Agnes.

This well is difficult to find now and, although it still runs freely, is hidden under trees. When my father was ninety-nine years young he told me that most people from the surrounding villages used to collect the water and, at one time, it was sold at tuppence a cup by a fishing family who inhabited a cottage next to the well. When the house fell into disrepair - which was inevitable because it was built too near the encroaching tides - the water was dispensed from a small wooden hut. Water from the 'holy well' was also barrelled and taken to Heysham, from where it was marketed as a 'cure-all' for holidaymakers. Take my dad's advice and leave the 'well' well alone or an upset tummy is on the cards and you may not be able to get to the nearest toilet quickly enough!

To the right of Humphrey Head and above Kents Bank is Kirkhead with its highest point the

Tower, from where the whole expanse of Morecambe Bay and beyond can be seen. During the Second World War the Tower was a lookout point for the 'Home Guard'. The Germans dropped a five hundred pound bomb in a field opposite Kirkhead Farm but the Army managed to defuse it safely the next day. There are still hollows in the ground as a result of enemy bombs in this area.

Grange-over-Sands faces south and is sheltered by Hampsfell Hospice which is seven hundred feet above sea level. To the north-east are the Howgills, the Pennines and hills of the Yorkshire Dales. It is all awe-inspiring to the walkers as most of them have never been before, but the highlight of the Morecambe Bay Walk still lies ahead.

After crossing several small dykes we arrive at the water's edge of the Kent. Today it is a wide expanse looking not so much like a river but a running sea! Not to worry as I have been across the previous day testing the depth and the firmness of the riverbed for the number of walkers. I also marked the safe route between branches of laurel. From the markers I can see that the river is now shallower - and this is reassuring to the group.

I line everyone up between the laurels and usually have a joke with them before crossing. Some, a little apprehensive at this wide stretch of water, soon gain confidence as I blow the whistle and take a forward position. We proceed slowly as I try my hardest to keep the group together.

If some are a little frightened, keeping close together gives them confidence and they start to enjoy the experience of a lifetime. Occasionally one or two people scream out, but not to worry as they are in no danger - they have trodden on a Morecambe Bay fluke. Some of the womenfolk almost jump out of their undies as they suddenly stand on something slippery about the size of a dinner plate. As the water deepens the pace slows down but it quickens again as it becomes shallow towards the Grange side, with the children and dogs racing to be the first on the other side.

This crossing must certainly be a magical experience for everyone taking part. We stand for a while, people chat, make new friends and even decide to take a snack or a drink from their rucksacks as I wait until the last person is on firm sand clear of the river before moving on. There is no hurry at this stage and there are lots of things to see and questions to be asked.

Over to our right is the village of Silverdale and at this point we can see the Furness Railway embankment and the viaduct over the River Kent, although Arnside is hidden from view. With Kents Bank station now in sight the pace quickens and, although I can walk with the best of them, this is not the right way to do it. I am responsible for everyone on the walk, especially those at the rear, so the whistle is blown and we all gather together, probably for the last time, before coming ashore at Kents Bank. After three hours we make our way over the marshy area and up onto terra firma.

Olive has come down with a friend by car and this is parked to meet us as we come in from a very enjoyable walk. A certificate and a copy of one of my books are available from the boot of the car, providing walkers with evidence to show their friends that they completed the trip safely. Afterwards, they can settle down comfortably at home and read all about it! Not everyone stops at the car to meet up with Olive, as they are in too much of a hurry to get to the nearest toilets, but they miss out on a treat. However, many do spare the time to have a chat and some ask for me to join them for a photograph before eventually returning home by car or coach.

The railway provides a much more direct route across the Kent estuary than the road, and thus is regularly used by walkers. Kents Bank station is almost swamped in this August 2002 scene by a large crown of walkers, who have completed the crossing and are waiting to return to Arnside by train. (John Briggs)

The 'people's choice'

As already mentioned, a more exciting walk now starts from the lovely seaside village of Arnside. Walkers taking this route keep along the foreshore with views towards Grange, Holme Island and Hampsfell before passing Arnside Coastguard station - of which I am an auxiliary member. Continuing towards Newbarns farmyard, they go through woodland and a caravan park to arrive at White Creek and onto the sands. This walk is more suitable for all age groups and that is why it has become so popular.

There is very little difference in mileage, although on the map it is only about four miles as the crow flies. We cannot fly so we go where it is safe - and that means a lot of meandering which adds to the mileage. The Sandpiper is always on hand out in the Bay for those who at any stage of the walk decide they cannot complete the journey to the shore. I find that the passengers on the trailer are usually young children - not because they are tired but because this is a novelty ride across Morecambe Bay. Enjoyment to the full!

Questions I am often asked

Very seldom does anyone ask questions at the start of a walk. People come up to me once we arrive on the sands, and always when we have stops out there to gather together.

1. *Can we ask you some questions, please?*
2. *Where are the quicksands?*
3. *Has anyone ever died out there?*
4. *Do you ever get frightened?*
5. *How do you know where to go and how did you learn this knowledge?*
6. *Have you ever been stuck in quicksands?*
7. *How deep is the river crossing?*
8. *How long have you been doing the walks?*
9. *Have you ever met the Queen?*
10. *Has Her Majesty ever been across the sands?*
11. *What time is low water?*
12. *At what time will the tide be here today?*
13. *Do you ever get fed up with leading the walks?*
14. *What will happen when you decide to call it a day?*

I answer all of these sensible and interesting questions in turn. Walkers seem to appreciate this, and I enjoy it too, as it appears to put them at ease.

Crossings in the Past

Centuries before the Morecambe Bay Walk as such was established, travellers were crossing the sands in order to shorten the distance to Furness. If all was well, the sand would be firm and the river fordable but a petition to the King from the Abbot of Furness in 1326 suggests that this was not often the case. He asked for a coroner to investigate the great loss of life on the sands.

The first record of a Guide is in 1501 when one Edmonstone was described as 'Carter-upon-Kent-Sands'. The Prior of Cartmel paid his successor, William Gate, although responsibility for payment later passed to Conishead Priory, near Ulverston. The future looked bleak, however, when the Abbot of Furness was charged with treason for involvement in the Pilgrimage of Grace in 1536. The dissolution of the monasteries followed almost at once and the vast Furness Abbey, the largest Cistercian foundation in the county, was surrendered with all its wealth. In 1540 its entire estates were transferred to the Duchy of Lancaster, which took on many of its obligations including payment for the Guide at Guide's Farm.

The earliest Duchy Patent dates from 1548 and granted Thomas Hodgson the office of Guide 'with one tenement in Kents-Bank in Cartmel, which was called Carte Hows, with three closes of land to the same adjacent'. For the next three hundred years succeeding generations of the Carter family came to hold the post and there is even a suggestion that the Hodgsons may have adapted the surname 'Carter' to cement their occupation identity.

It does seem weird to write about the previous Guides in terms of office - all of whom lived at Guide's Farm and sat in the same room where this book has been written. What did they think about being a Guide? Did they realise how important it was? They would not have believed so many people could have crossed the Bay in the last forty years.

Why so many of the earlier Guides were described as 'Carters of the Sands' is difficult to determine. Their duty was to be in attendance at the fords, which they were bound to discover on the ebb tide, and conduct persons across safely. It appears that the Guides used to have a horse and cart at the edge of the rivers to convey foot passengers. This must have been more comfortable than wading through water with a strong current, especially in the winter months when the rivers would be icy cold. Horsemen were seldom able to cross without taking their feet out of the stirrups and raising them to escape a wetting. Those who were particular about the condition of their stirrups lifted them out of their saddles to prevent the salt water ruining them!

Many famous people have crossed the Bay. In 1759 the evangelist John Wesley made the journey, as did George Fox, the celebrated founder of the Quakers - the Society of Friends. Thomas Gray (1716- 1771), one of the greatest English poets and the writer of the famous 'Elegy in a Country Churchyard', crossed the sands twice, once in 1767 and again in 1769 on tours of the Lake District.

An enquiry was held at Grange in April 1873 as to the suitability of John Nevison, the then Guide, and whether it was worth continuing the appointment in view of the declining cross-sands traffic. At the hearing, which found in favour of retention, it was alleged that Nevison 'often spent whole days drinking at Dickinson's public house at Allithwaite'.

Guides from 1501

Edmondstone	1501	(1)
William Gate	1535	(2)
Thomas Hodgson	1548	
Richard Carter	? – 1564	(3)
William Carter	1564–1592	
William Carter	1592 – 1602	
Edward Carter	1602 – 1633	
Edward Carter	1633 1644	
William Carter	1644 – 1649	
Thoma Carter	1649 – 1661	(4)
William Carter	1661 – 1672	(5)
J Carter	?	
John Carter	c1680 – 1718	
John Carter	1718 – 1746	
John Carter	1746 – 1780	
John Carter	1780 – 1799	
William Carter	1800 – 1828	
James Carter	1828 – 1856	
John Carter	1856 – 1867	
John Nevison	1867 – 1875	(6)
George Sedgwick	1875 – 1919	
Jack Burrow	1919 – 1943	
Jack Burrow	1943 – 1950	(7)
William Burrow	1950 – 1963	
Cedric Robinson	1963 –	

1. 'Carter upon Kent Sands'
2. Paid by the Prior of Cartmel
3. Name possibly taken from, the place where he lived- 'Carter House'
4. In 1660 guided the people taking George Fox to prison
5. Drowned in the course of his duty
6. Dismissed
7. Son of former guide

Famous Occasions

Had the decision of the 1873 enquiry gone the other way, it is interesting to reflect that I would not have been able to write this book. Nor would I have had the pleasure of guiding many famous people across the sands. The most memorable occasion occurred in 1985.

The Duke of Edinburgh

May 30th 1985 was for me a very special crossing as I accompanied the Duke of Edinburgh in the royal carriage, along with ten other horse-drawn carriages following close behind on the only route possible at that time. This was from Silverdale to Kents Bank, with the Duke driving a magnificent team of four horses to a sturdy Marathon vehicle.

I had guided thousands of people across Morecambe Bay but this was something totally different from any crossing before. A great deal of preparation went into this event so that everything would run as smoothly as possible. The sands and the River Kent were unstable with constant movement but eventually they did settle down to make the crossing feasible. There were press interviews at Holker Hall, the home of Lord and Lady Cavendish and family, and at Kents Bank Hotel and Guide's Farm as well as several meetings with the Lancashire and Cumbria police forces. The organisers had to keep the whole occasion under wraps until it was officially announced from Buckingham Palace that the Duke would be taking part and it was really going to happen, as this was one man's decision.

After going out onto the sands very early at 3.30am to make a final check before the crossing in the afternoon, I was very pleased with what I found and turned for home as the sun rose, knowing that we were in for a perfect day. I had now made my decision for the drive to go ahead and it was all systems go! It was a truly memorable event, not just for Olive, myself and our family and friends, but for all the thousands of people who turned out on the day to watch this historic occasion.

Lord Bragg

It started with a phone call from Melvyn Bragg's London office asking if it would be possible for me to accompany him on a walk across the Bay. A date was chosen and we were to meet up at Morecambe Lodge Farm at Bolton-le-Sands, very near to Hest Bank railway station.

My daughter Jean drove me round to the other side of the Bay and, as we arrived, we noticed a parked vehicle. A figure stepped out and came towards me as I was preparing myself for the walk, changing into trainers as the sand looked hard and dry at the start. I did not recognise Melvyn at first as he was wearing casual clothes - trainers and a pair of jeans and looked nothing like he appeared when seen on television. A few words were exchanged - yes, this was Melvyn and now we were both ready for the crossing.

It was a glorious day for the walk over to Kents Bank. As the high sun hit the sand, you could

Melvyn Bragg and Cedric setting out across the Bay from Hest Bank in May 1985. (Leslie Stringer)

scarcely bear to look. It was like a sheet of silver spread out across the open Bay. The gulls, oystercatchers and the singing cockles were all to be seen and heard on this most beautiful mid-May afternoon by just the two of us. The Lakeland fells were clearly visible and at their best and we would see lots more as this was to be a four-hour journey. With the breeze coming from the south-west the clouds soon cleared and left us with lovely blue skies so that which ever way we looked it was as pretty as a picture.

Melvyn asked me questions continually and my main topic was fishing and the pleasure of it, but we also discussed the Bay and the sands themselves. I was able to explain where new channels were about to be formed, where 'bracks' (breakaways of sand in the rivers and dykes) were suspect, where quicksands threatened and the sad stories of loss of life. The reason Melvyn wished to accompany me on a walk was to get the sensation of being on the Bay, which he wanted to convey in a book he was about to write entitled The Maid of Buttermere. He could not have come on a more ideal day and I did enjoy his company.

Although my estimate of the crossing time was four hours, it did in fact take us five and a half with the continual stopping to ask questions and look around. The River Kent was awesome, very wide and almost thigh deep. Melvyn is not quite as tall as I am but we both got a wetting, although we soon dried out in the warm sun and the breeze. At the finish as we came up towards the railway station, Melvyn thanked me and said how much he had enjoyed the experience, but he was certainly tired and his legs were beginning to ache. He told me that when he was up in the Lakes he walked the fells and regarded himself as fit, but walking the sands was something he would never forget.

Melvyn later wrote an article in Punch about his experience of crossing the sands, from which the following extract is taken:

'There are people you meet who come straight out of a book, even in our sophisticated times when such a nice and simple phrase might seem rarer than a Nigerian Turnip, even in our television age (when actually more books are read, but let that pass) when we are collectively accused of reneging on the fine print. Even so, these people exist, only sometimes as 'characters' and they can step out of the pages and into your life without so much as a (book) token of acknowledgement, of the difference between life and fiction.

I met a man the other day. He led me across the sands of Morecambe Bay. Cedric Robinson is the Queen's Guide to the Sands, but also takes the title of Sand Pilot. It is a title which evokes the ancient and the romantic. Pilot has been an inspiration, a metaphor, a hope.

Tennyson - 'I hope to see my Pilot face to face when I have crossed the bar' and those who bear that title inherit an ancient Kingdom of Trust. You feel some of that as you trudge out across the Morecambe Bay Sands.

When Wordsworth resettled in the Lakes on Christmas Eve, 1799, it was a place in which those binding nourishing rural communities and those open plain but heroic people who are the most cherished characters, and in his work could still be found. For Wordsworth they had links with Arcadia, and with the deep decency of an honest endeavour which encountered the largest claims with stoicism and drear sustenance, even Solace from nature. 'Michael' is the most vivid of these creations - a shepherd whose only son abandoned him for the corrupting city and left him without an heir, without hope, stricken down but always a man of worth.

I suspect that Cedric Robinson would find such an introduction and such a comparison embarrassing, but it is there. If you know the Lakes and knew Wordsworth then you have met him before and he does not let you down. Even his turn of phrase reaches back 'And it was done And so we did' - while his appearance, strong, thatched grey hair, cheeks apple ripe with the weather, movement at once steady and alert - comes straight from resolution and independence.'

Bill Bryson

When you meet Bill Bryson you soon feel that you have known him all your life. He is so friendly and approachable and laid back, but he is also very witty. The plan was for Bill and his TV crew to join me on the shore at Kents Bank for a walk with a small group of excited locals. It was a nice clear day but there was a very cold wind. Bill told me that he never felt entirely comfortable with British seaside weather, even on the sunniest of days in summer, so I arranged for my nephew Kenny to have my tractor and Sandpiper trailer at the ready to give them more confidence.

Bill said that he grew up almost a thousand miles from the nearest sea and the reason why he liked Morecambe Bay so much was that it was compact and pretty. Much of the time there was not much water in it at all - and that was his kind of bay! One other thing he found hard to understand was why so many people just sat on the edge of the Bay. It was certain to be chilly and damp and a long way from toilets, and there was nothing to do but huddle behind a windbreak and gaze out into a cold grey sea.

Bill had a conversation with one of the group, a nice man who had retired into Grange from Rochdale. He was wearing a pair of low-cut shoes with socks and carrying a thumb-stick. He enjoyed talking to Bill and, as he had been on the sands with me before, he described the sands and the river crossing so well that you would have thought that he had known them all his life.

"There is always one!" commented Bill. They are there to tell you that what you are about to do is not as you imagined. The River Kent could in fact be at least three hundred yards across and come well up to your knees if you are lucky - and can be much deeper - and so amazingly these people always carry a stick. On the other hand, and he would be corrected if he were wrong, he had been looking forward to this walk so much today - until he was given my book Sand Pilot of Morecambe Bay. Some words in the book put doubt in his mind as he read, "Across the sands of Morecambe Bay the tide advances faster than a man can run, quicksands and ever-changing channels have in the past claimed countless lives. And now it is not uncommon for holidaymakers to find themselves in difficulty."

The doubt in his mind changed when I spoke to the group and this seemed to give him more confidence. It was to be quite a while before we met up with the River Kent. As we walked we chatted, stopped occasionally and filmed, and he thought it odd to reflect that a few hours earlier the spot where we were now walking had been under at least twenty feet of water. The one disappointment was that we could not walk straight across the Bay to Morecambe because of deep water! Too deep to wade and too wide to swim, so now instead we had to turn left towards Arnside and the Kent. Here at last was what everyone had been waiting for - the river crossing.

From here it looks positively enormous and very, very wide. I jokingly shouted ahead to the group, "Any non-swimmers?" The tractor was alongside us just in case. Bill had very few rules in life, so he said, but one of them was - never wade across a body of water when you could not see to the other side. Another was - never immerse yourself in anything colder than liquid nitrogen.

As we walked into the river I could not stop myself from laughing as I saw the look on most of the group's faces. Bill said he could feel his bones cracking and the odd pained numbness with the sensation that his toes were about to fall off. Someone in the group spoke and Bill said, "He didn't really say that this was lovely, did he?" When we arrived safely at the other side, Bill took the shoulder of someone so as not to lose his balance, emptied out the water from his wellies and then put them back on again!

We now took a line for White Creek, which was the last leg of the sand journey. This took us about twenty minutes. As we walked up towards Newbarn's Caravan Park and on to much higher ground, we looked back over the way we had come and it was so clear that the views were really outstanding. Crossing the Kent was now the topic of conversation and everyone of us had a good laugh when Bill told us that the producer was probably sitting quite comfortably in a warm pub somewhere in Arnside waiting for us!

Bishop of Liverpool

One of my walks in 2006 was organised by the Bishop of Liverpool as part of his 'Right to Life' campaign. It was agreed over the phone with Olive that the Bishop and his secretary would pay us a visit to discuss the details and a date and time were fixed. I was in the living room at about that time and, looking out of the window, I saw a couple coming up the path towards the doorway. I said to Olive, "I think the Bishop and his secretary have arrived." So she rushed to open the front door, shook the man's hand and, looking pleased with herself, said: "Oh, I'm very pleased to meet you." The man looked at her in amazement, and then Olive asked, "You are the Bishop of Liverpool aren't you?"

"No dear," he replied, "I have only called for half a dozen eggs!" We all had a good laugh about and it was only a matter of minutes later that the Bishop and his secretary arrived.

Two well known government ministers took part in the walk with the Bishop. They were Anne Widdecombe and Lord Halton, and they said they had enjoyed it and would certainly like to come again.

Film & TV

There was now wide interest by television companies interested in filming out there in Morecambe Bay. It is the perfect location and most of the time - weather permitting - is surely a photographer's dream. There are few places in the world to equal the Bay with its beautiful sunrises and sunsets, ever changing sands and fascinating tides. There are also quicksands...

The 'body' on the sands

Professor Magnus Pike was on television with a programme called 'Don't Ask Me'. Members of the audience could put questions about almost anything and some bright spark asked him, "What makes quicksands?" No expense was spared and the programme was filmed by Yorkshire Television. This is going back some years and the young and very enthusiastic producer at that time was Barry Cockcroft, whom my wife Olive and I came to know quite well over the years.

At first a researcher, a young lass of no more than about twenty years of age, came along to Guide's Farm to find out just what these quicksands were all about. I took her over Cart Lane railway crossing and down onto the foreshore after she had donned a pair of Olive's green wellies. I explained as much as I could and then asked if she was game for it. She replied, "That's why I am here Mr Robinson." So I took her by the hand, said "don't stop whatever", and, as the surface of the sand bent and buckled, and showed signs of cracking open, we raced across and onto firm terrain. She said afterwards how really frightened she had been but thought that this would make a very good film. And it did.

Television and film companies regularly come to Morecambe Bay to record celebrities completing the walk or to make educational productions and documentaries. Here members of a film unit are clinging gamely to Cedric's tractor as they come ashore at Kents Bank. (Fred Broomfield)

A lot went into the making of the film, including a rescue attempt by a very large orange coloured air-sea rescue helicopter. It was difficult lifting the man from the sands even with all that power and at one stage the procedure did not go according to plan. The suction was so great that the rope slung around the victim's arms was pulling the helicopter down, which was really frightening to watch. Then, all of a sudden, release, and up he came slowly - and the helicopter made its way across the Bay and back towards Yorkshire with a man dangling on the end of a rope!

That is not the end of the story - oh no! After the experts back at Yorkshire Television studios had studied the film, they decided that the man had not gone down far enough into the quicksands and thus it did not look sufficiently dangerous. So they rang me and told me this! They could not get anyone else to take part in the film by walking over the quicksands as word had got around as to how hazardous they were! I suggested to them that they should make a dummy and, as long as it was heavy enough, it should sink quite easily.

The second visit with the dummy went perfectly. The lower half from the waist was made of steel and the upper parts of wood and it looked almost real. It had to be held so that it did not topple, so I volunteered and laid down flat over the quicksands just out of camera shot. Down he went, up to the waist, as the camera rolled and everyone watching was so pleased. The shoots from this scene were put together with the earlier ones, edited, and were a great success.

The only thing now was that the camera crew were all safely back in Yorkshire and there was a 'man' stuck in the quicksands! Almost every household in Kents Bank and Grange has clear views of the Bay, so our telephone was now ringing non-stop with callers very worried about what they could see out there as the tide was coming in.

I said to Olive, "This has got to stop!" So as the tide ebbed, I took my old bushman saw out of the shed and, after giving Olive a kiss and her telling me to be very careful, I went down the lane, over the railway crossing and onto the sands. The man was still there - he had not moved a jot. I got wet through laying flat down on to the sands, gritted my teeth and started sawing him off by his waist.

Coming back safely up the shore, I felt really good about what I had just done. At least now the phone would stop ringing about the 'man' in the quicksands, but just imagine someone walking their dog along the shoreline one day and suddenly coming across part of a body washed up by the tide. It could have proved very frightening - but I never heard of anything being found.

"Cut, Mr Robinson!"

In October 1974 I had quite a part to play in a film called 'Lakeland Summer' which was shown on BBC TV's 'Pebble Mill at One'. My role was to re-enact a Guide in the past and to forsake my old tractor for one of my favourite ponies - a palomino gelding. The idea was to be filmed on horseback marking out the route and guiding a team of horses pulling a very old-fashioned carriage across the sands to Grange.

Cheyenne, my pony, was quite a handful when he was unloaded from the horsebox on the foreshore at Morecambe Lodge Farm, near Hest Bank. He was like a two-year old and would not stand still while being saddled up. On our way over the sands to the place we were to start the filming he bucked all the way!

I was to mark the route with laurel bushes, but whenever I dismounted and worked one into the sand Cheyenne walked forward, got hold with his teeth and out came the bush! He showed me up continually. The direction from the producer was now quite frequent, "Cut, Mr Robinson, can we have that scene again please." Yes, I have some treasured memories of being filmed out on the Bay. Bob Langley was the interviewer and he rode across in style in that lovely old carriage.

It was nice to hear again from BBC TV in February 1975 with news that 'Lakeland Summer' had been a huge success. A repeat programme was to be shown and would go out as three twenty-five minute films in April. I thought this was great, but never in a million years did I ever want to be a budding actor and stand in front of a television camera with lots of unrehearsed questions to be answered. However, I was now beginning to enjoy the set-up and provided it was about the sands or something connected with them, I was quite happy to go along with whatever they suggested.

'Sand Pilot'

My first book Sand Pilot of Morecambe Bay was published in 1980 and Olive and I, my whole family, neighbours and friends were thrilled to bits over it. A respectable person from Grange had told me in conversation that this just did not happen unless you were well known. Me, being green as grass, thought that anyone could get a script published, without any problems. Anyway, maybe I was lucky and I proved them wrong, but the publishers were well pleased and gave it plenty of publicity nationally.

Lots of signing sessions were organised for me to attend and the first was at the station bookstall in Grange. I was sat there enjoying myself and things were going really well when a call came through from Granada Television at Manchester. They wanted me to travel to their studios and would provide a taxi there and back. Times of arrival were given to me and I was told my interviewer would be Bob Smithies. I could not wait to tell Olive about this and she and all the family were only too pleased for me to go.

I had not previously met Bob Smithies and did not know what to expect. The temperature inside so hot that I could feel my face getting redder and redder by the minute. Bob did not waste much time after the handshake and led me to the powder room. When he opened the door I could not help but notice well-known names such as Elsie Tanner written above the dressing table mirrors. "Take a seat," said Bob, "anywhere will do" - so I sat in front of one of those large mirrors. Bob did the same, but I think he had his own special chair.

The next thing I knew we were both being made up to appear before the television cameras. I needed much more make-up than Bob because by this time you could have boiled a kettle on my head! I was powdered, eyebrows trimmed and sticking-out bits lopped from my hair. I emerged looking like and feeling like a circus clown!

All seemed to go to plan and I came home to a wonderful surprise party that Olive and family had organised for me. They had invited our good friends and neighbours so there was quite a house full. She had made a special cake in the shape of an open book with the title across the top icing. We all had more than a happy hour, a really great time with such a lovely buffet. It was a memorable send off for the new book.

When Cedric's first book Sand Pilot of Morecambe Bay was published in 1980, the whole family, friends and neighbours were 'thrilled to bits over it'. A special celebration included a suitably iced cake.

A new edition of Sand Pilot of Morecambe Bay in 1998 included a foreword by Hannah Hauxwell, who accompanied Cedric to the signing sessions. They took time out for a walk along the foreshore at Kents Bank, and are also seen in the group photograph at Guide's Farm along with Olive and Lavinia Thwaites – Hannah's good friend from her village of Cotherstone in Teesdale. (Fred Broomfield)

The second meeting with Bob was an invitation for us both to attend a dinner given by Granada Television at the Tythe Barn Restaurant at Garstang where we met many TV celebrities. Bob has now retired from television but a few years ago he rang and asked if it would be possible for me to accompany him, his wife and a few friends on a walk across the Bay from Arnside to Kents Bank which, of course, I agreed to do. The walk was at a relaxing pace and, with being just a few of us, we were able to walk and talk and even stop from time to time to take photographs. The day was just perfect for us and we could not have enjoyed ourselves more.

When Sand Pilot of Morecambe Bay was republished in 1998, Hannah Hauxwell wrote a new foreword. She had become a good friend as a result of earlier visits to Kents Bank when on holiday, but now she stayed with us for a week and accompanied Olive and me to all the signing sessions, which she enjoyed. We also travelled to Radio Blackburn and the two of us broadcast live on the same subject. At the time there was a heavy snowfall and I was hoping and praying that it would not last. Luckily it disappeared almost as fast as it came down and we were able to travel home in safety.

Many people both locally and on my travels ask about Hannah Hauxwell. Is she still alive? How old will she be now? Well, I can tell you, she is keeping well and had her eightieth birthday on August 1st, 2006. We still keep in touch with her and one day I will go and pick her up and bring her to Guide's Farm for a holiday. Like many celebrities, Grange-over-Sands is a place she loves to visit. The town has the mildest climate in the North West thanks to its location by the Gulf Stream and the sheltering mountains.

Sir Harry Secombe

By the early 1980s there was more interest than ever in making short films centred on the Bay. Border Television arranged for me to be filmed with Sir Harry Secombe for the programme 'Highway - Morecambe Bay'. He was one of the nicest persons one could ever wish to meet. In August 1989 I had to provide filming facilities for the cross-Bay walk from Arnside to Kents Bank and, if it turned out to be wet, we would film early in September. Later in September I was to have my tractor and trailer at Kents Bank station to take part in various sequences to be included in the programme.

Harry rang me from Kents Bank on the day we were about to be filmed saying that he had done his stint - and now it was my turn so could I get down to the station as soon as possible! When I arrived he was standing at the door of a vehicle about the size of a caravan. He beckoned me over and said, "Come inside, Cedric, sit yourself down" There were several people in the van who were all introduced to me. Harry asked, "How's the old eye doing Cedric?" - he knew I had had an operation for a detached retina. When I replied that it seemed to be doing nicely, he surprised me by saying, "Oh but don't be too sure about that Cedric. I have a good pal who had the same operation and he has been falling over himself ever since." When I asked who it was, he smiled and then replied, "Spike Milligan." I took him to be serious, but he was just pulling my leg!

We travelled out onto the sands in Sandpiper, my tractor-drawn covered trailer driven by my good friend Larry. Despite the very windy weather on that day, filming went well and it was such a pleasure to be out on the sands in the company of Sir Harry Secombe.

More personalities

There have been many other visits by film crews down the years. Two very well known TV personalities, Victoria Wood and 'Hayley' from Coronation Street, crossed the sands under my guidance. Victoria was accompanied by a minder and wore a peaked hat well down over her eyes so that she would not be recognised. Haley was not so cautious and made friends with everyone. After the walk was over she obliged many people by signing her autograph or even having a photograph taken with them. This was a sponsored walk to raise money to help fight Parkinson's Disease as Hayley's father was a sufferer.

Alistair Macdonald, regularly on TV at one time with Stuart Hall, was the first interviewer to come all the way across the Bay together with a camera crew who filmed the walk. It was a perfect day for it. We started out from Hest Bank and finished on the promenade at Grange.

The long-running holiday programme 'Wish you were here' with Judith Chalmers was filmed from Kents Bank and out in the Bay. Judith and her entourage travelled around to this side of the Bay from Morecambe after being filmed on the funfair. Out we went onto the sands with my tractor and trailer until we came to the River Kent, where the crew lost no time in setting up their gear. There was a cameraman, the soundman, two or three other blokes who just seemed to walk back and forth to the tractor and trailer, and the continuity person. You learn a lot from these people when you are out with them quite frequently. The filming went extraordinarily well, with Judith being well pleased with herself after chasing me up and down in the river, or was it the other way round? It is so long ago since the filming took place that I am not quite so sure!

Another of my visits out onto the sands to be filmed was in October 1987 in the interesting company of David Bellamy. It was for a Yorkshire Television children's programme called 'Bellamy's Bugle'.

'Blue Peter' was one of the first programmes to be filmed in the Bay with Simon Groom driving my tractor. Goldie, their dog, loved being out on the sands as it was quite a change for him not to be filmed in the studio.

'Treasure Hunt' was filmed in Morecambe Bay from a helicopter. I was driven out to the location on a horse-drawn carriage, the area chosen being about four miles out from Kents Bank. Anneka Rice was not available for this series so Anabelle Croft took her place. George Bowman from Penrith came down with his team of horses, which took part in the filming. The helicopter did eventually find us out in the Bay and I had previously marked out a circle with laurels where it was safe for it to land. I had to hide the clue in the sand, marked with a laurel twig. Anabelle had to enlist my help in finding the clue, once down on the sands, but as the studio contestants guided her around the course it was difficult for me to know her exact time of arrival. Eventually I was spotted and filming went ahead as planned

On another occasion I was again being filmed for television and this time the interviewer was Paul Heiney. Morecambe Bay was shown from a different angle, as I was filmed leaving Grange by Crown Hill and taking the footpath known as Bailey Lane. This leads you very steeply down to the railway crossing and promenade and out onto the sands. The only thing was that the cameraman had to be a few paces in front of me and walking backwards, which must have been very difficult for him. I kept thinking to myself, "Any minute now and he'll fall over himself." But he didn't, and we carried on to do the interview out in the Bay.

In April 1995 I was asked if I would take part in a documentary film about the Marijushri Mahayana Buddhist Centre at Conishead Priory, near Ulverston. It was a very early hour in the morning when filming took place out in the Bay near Chapel Island and it was very cold. I was with two Buddhists who were wearing only their thin wraps and must have been starved to death.

As we came ashore we were interviewed at great length, and I was glad to get back into the car and warm myself up. After a few months I was sent a finished videotape, which they called 'The Guide', together with a letter of thanks. All of us at Guide's Farm found the video most interesting.

I had often watched Fred, the TV Weatherman, jump across the water and land on the floating map of the British Isles, sometimes almost falling in! He came to Grange in February 1997 and drove his favourite little red bubble car along the promenade where we met and were filmed together. In May the same year I was recorded on video for the archives of the British History Trust.

Visiting celebrities: David Bellamy (top left) with Olive and Cedric; Judith Chalmers, with Cedric's grandson Simon, during the filming of 'Wish You Were Here' (bottom left); Alistair Macdonald, who in 1982 was the first interviewer to come all the way across the Bay with a camera crew (top right); Russell Harty (bottom right), with Barbara Stothart and Cedric, after coming ashore at Arnside. (Fred Broomfield)

I was again filmed in July by American TV to show the dangers of quicksands out in the Bay. Their interviewer was Eric Strauss who had a really strong American accent. When filming was over it was suggested that we ail went out for a meal to the 'Guide over Sands' public house at Allithwaite. I had previously been invited by the brewery to pull the first pint at this newly renovated pub, which used to be called 'The Royal Oak'. That evening we all had a first-class meal.

Visits by television companies interested in filming out in the Bay still continue. Maybe not quite as often as they used to, but the programme 'Coast of Britain' has been shown on TV on several occasions. My small contribution focused on the quicksands of the Bay. The programme was so enjoyable and I was delighted to take part.

The quicksands were also explored in a BBC series 'Coast', a thirteen-part documentary that featured Morecambe Bay when it looked at the coastline from Liverpool to Carlisle. I discussed the dangers of the Bay with Neil Oliver and also appearing was geographer and writer Nicholas Crane.

In September 2006 the TV company Bakermedia invited me to meet them on the other side of the Bay at Silverdale to film the high tides. On a second occasion they filmed out in the Bay from Kents Bank. The interviewer was Dean Sullivan of 'Brookside' fame and the programme was scheduled to be shown in spring 2007 under the title 'My North West'.

A very well known actor Ian McKellan, seen in the film 'Lord of the Rings', came to Guide's Farm to take part in a BBC TV documentary 'Go North West'. I didn't have to take part in the production, only to transport him and the film crew out into the most suitable place in the Bay whilst I looked on.

Later that day I was out in the Bay from Kents Bank with a different film crew, who put together a TV series 'My North West' for transmission in spring 2007. It centred round a man of the hills who is seventy years young and has walked and climbed most of the Lakeland fells. The producer came up with the idea of him meeting up with the man of the sands and getting us together. It was an amazing experience and we hit it off with one another right away. A week later Olive and I received a most beautiful arrangement of flowers, with a message that read: 'From the man of the hills to the man and woman of the sands.' What a wonderful thought!

Horses and carriages crossing the railway at Kents Bank before heading out into the Bay

Riders Across the Bay

Until the royal carriage crossing of the sands by the Duke of Edinburgh in 1985 there had been very little interest in crossing the Bay, either on horseback or horse-drawn carriages. I believe that this was the first crossing of its kind for over one hundred years.

Judge Sir Sanderson Temple, known to most people as Sandy, lived over the other side of the Bay and was a really grand person. So approachable and down-to-earth, he was also a very clever man. He was a keen horseman, a good rider and enjoyed driving his horse and carriage. I believe he had ridden in point-to-point races in his younger days. Sandy, his sister Barbara Stothart and my family and friends volunteered to help with the royal carriage crossing and so this made it much easier for me. Sandy took part in the crossing, driving his own turnout, and sat at his side was Lord Cavendish of Holker Hall.

I have always been a keen horse lover and at this time owned a pedigree fell pony. As a first step, I had him up and down the roads dragging a car tyre with a huge chain wrapped around to make a lot of noise. He wasn't the slightest bit worried and seemed to enjoy it. Next I rang my cousin, Jennifer Snell, who lives in Ulverston. She had won many rosettes at the local show with her own pony and so she gave me lots of encouragement. She couldn't have been more helpful, and she drove through to Guide's Farm with her horsebox, bringing a lovely trap for Chester. We then yoked up and I drove him along the lane, with Jennifer and her husband Maurice keeping close by with a leading rein just in case, but he was a natural. I was sorry that I didn't keep this up and take him further, but we always seemed too busy here at the farm, mostly with me out on the sands and Olive always answering the phone.

Sandy rang with an idea for me taking horses and carriages across the Bay to raise money for riding for the disabled, which I agreed to and so gave him a date. I thought I would mention my own horse Chester to him. He immediately said, "Bring him over here and we will put him in the cart for you." I was sorry I didn't take him up on his very generous offer, but soon afterwards Chester became ill with Lymes disease. Deer come into the fields and he had picked up a tick. Eventually, after being treated by the vet, he lost his battle for life and had to be put to sleep to prevent further suffering. We bought him as a four year old and he was ten years old when he died.

We all shed tears over the sad loss of such a good pony. We are attached to all our animals. Even strangers walking along the footpath alongside the field in which he grazed were anxious about him. One nice couple from Grange-over-Sands came along every week to feed him a few carrots, and when he died they were so upset that at a later date they came along with a tribute to him. They had typed this out so neatly. It was all about Chester and his lovely ways.

It was quite a while since Sandy had asked me if it was possible to take the carriage drive across the Bay and he hadn't come back to me to confirm the numbers so I decided that I would give him a ring. It was getting close to the day of the event and I always like to know beforehand how many will be taking part. He said, "Cedric, I believe there's a hundred carriages coming tomorrow!"

When I arrived at Newbarns Farm, Arnside, to meet up with Sandy and his followers, I was pleased with what I saw. Not the hundred carriages that Sandy had mentioned but sixty-seven horse riders and three carriages all being saddled up and preparing to cross the sands. Weatherwise it was rather miserable with misty rain, and the drive was to start at 2.30pm across the Bay to Kents Bank and back again to Arnside. The River Kent wasn't at its best so I was pleased that there were more horse riders than carriages.

Sandy had told me earlier that he had broken two 'zonkeys' to harness. These were a cross between a zebra and a donkey and he had been really excited about driving this team across the Bay, but one of them had gone down whilst driving out on the country lanes and had a cut on a foreleg, so it was now out of action. The other zonkey was offered to a helper of Sandy's to be ridden across the Bay. Although he took up the offer, he had never previously ridden in a saddle. When we arrived at Kents Bank shore, he had to be lifted from his mount and he was so sore and stiff that you could have a got a wheelbarrow between his legs. The worst thing was he had to ride this zonkey all the way back again to Arnside.

It was a really wonderful experience for everyone except this poor chap who will probably never want to sit in the saddle again. It was close to dusk when we arrived back at Arnside, where the riding horses were being put back in their boxes. I had a chat with Sandy as he and his helpers unyoked his beautifully turned out grey mare and gave her a feed. It was almost like looking back in the past, out there on those sands on that wet and misty day. It was the way they came in the days before the opening of the railway in 1857, but sadly many never made it across the Bay.

There are very few places left in this world today where one can get away from it all, but we have it here on our own doorstep. Horse riders and their mounts, as well as carriage drivers with their assorted turnouts, come annually to Morecambe Bay to escape from the ever increasing traffic and congested roads.

Phylis, a very experienced rider, rings me each year and I give her two dates. From these she chooses the best day weatherwise, usually in August. She comes with some twenty riders, some from West Craven Bridle Club and the Lancashire Group, and others from the Furness area. A number of those taking part in this ride have been before and just love the experience of being out there, galloping at speed and splashing through the shallows and the deeper River Kent.

The horse Phyllis rides is rather special and is a Spanish breed, very fast with lots of stamina. She intended to book a riding holiday in Spain. Then she saw an advert in a Scottish paper concerning a woman who had lived in the Borders and had recently brought five horses over from Spain. So she did the next best thing and booked a riding holiday in Scotland, where she had the pleasure of riding out on one of this special breed. Phyllis was so taken with it that she asked the owner if she would be prepared to sell it to her, and so this is now the horse that she rides out into the Bay each year.

I do not ride any more, but I have a good friend, Brian Proctor from Rathmell, near Settle, who comes here with his good looking, quiet and sensible grey gelding and carriage. We lead the way, through dykes and watery areas and then on to the highlight, the crossing of the River Kent. Both horses and their riders seem to love the experience. We always stop for a well deserved break at White Creek, a beautiful inlet where, on low tides with fine weather, the sand is hard and dry. We are met with one of the riding club's senior members, who has come along from Arnside with flasks of coffee, tea, soft drinks and usually chocolate, which she hands out to everyone whilst the horses take a breather. Riders now mingle and it is interesting to listen to what they have to say about this unusual experience and what memories they will take home with them to tell their friends and families.

Eventually it is time to head back the way we came, with Brian driving his grey horse and with

The end of a cross-Bay carriage drive, with members of the Ribble Valley Driving Club coming ashore at Kents Bank. (Fred Broomfield)

me sitting alongside. Through the River Kent, on and on, walking and trotting, with the riders sometimes holding their mounts back and then coming at full gallop towards us like a stampede. We arrive back at Kents Bank where the horses are fed, groomed and boxed. Saddles and gear are washed off ready for their next adventure, but it will be another year before they cross the Bay again.

Ribble Valley Driving Club has been coming into the area now for quite a number of years, with me taking them on a drive across the sands if weather and conditions permit. We have in the past driven over the Leven sands to Chapel Island, but much more exciting for everyone is to be able to drive across the bay to Arnside, the White Creek area and back again to Kents Bank.

The club is a family affair, with youngsters involved and people joining from all walks of life. It is a hobby rather than competitive driving and they have several camps during the year. One of these is at Cartmel racecourse, but the available dates don't always fall on a week when tides are right. On these occasions we still go out into the Bay for a drive. There is nothing to equal a carriage crossing of Morecambe Bay on a suitable day, with horses of all types and colours splashing through the river at breakneck speed, their drivers and passengers getting soaked to the skin and all enjoying the experience to the full. It is a sight to see and one most certainly never forgotten.

Horse riders and carriage drivers with their assorted turnouts find Morecambe Bay a wonderful place to experience freedom and escape from the pressures of modern living. The photographs on this and the following pages capture the pleasure and sheer exhilaration of it all.

Crossings with a Difference

Many of my most memorable crossings have not involved celebrities but nevertheless have been equally interesting and rewarding.

The Battle of White Creek

A walk that I led across the Bay in June 1974 stands out in my mind as being the most colourful I have ever recorded. I received a letter from the Roundheads' Association asking me to lead an army of Cavaliers across the sands to White Creek, Arnside, where they were to meet up and do battle with the Roundheads in the first re-enactment of its kind.

The Cavaliers assembled over on the shore, at Cart Lane, crossing before moving out in style across the Bay. The day was beautiful and so were the women's costumes - pretty bonnets, blouses of various colours and style, with long white cotton skirts and leather footwear. The men, being soldiers, were in full battle uniform with their lances held upright and were wearing long boots made in leather. I thought it was a pity to cross the sands, and especially the River Kent, as their beautiful costumes would never be the same again once they had gone through the water.

A good friend of mine, Mrs Hirst, asked if she could come along on this special day and watch the battle. Our daughter Jean and her friend Deirdre went with her for company.

The crossing went wonderfully well, in a military kind of style, on the approach to White Creek. Hidden from view were the Roundheads and their sign for battle to commence was some very loud cannon fire. Mrs Hirst, Jean, Deirdre and I all ran for cover and watched from a distance - a very safe one as now all hell was let loose with such a noise. People were screaming and shouting and it was a pitched battle that went on for some time.

From where we stood, this battle certainly looked for real and some of them did get hurt. We never did find out who won because it became time for me and my three onlookers to make our way back across the river before the tide turned. Coming ashore at Cart Lane, Mrs Hirst was so thrilled at being able to cross the sands and record this colourful event on camera that she gave me a set of photographs that I still treasure.

Under sail

In September 1974 I received a letter asking me to accompany a man and his Chinese Wheelbarrow, or Desert Cart, from one side of the Bay to the other - a distance of about nine or ten miles, depending on which way the wind is blowing. It was a lightweight affair with a wheel five feet in diameter and a long narrow box on either side to carry the load.

The distribution of the load in this way put the weight on the cart and not on the driver. A sail was used to take advantage of any favourable wind, leaving only the guiding of the cart to the driver and enabling him to cover many more miles than would have been the case had he had to push or pull the load of a conventional cart.

The whole idea was to test the cart in the stringent conditions of the Bay before taking it out to the Sahara Desert for a further test, after which it was hoped to put it into production. It was seen as a potential benefit to desert people, who could not afford to use motorised transport or camels to move their wares. The vehicle was to be manufactured by a well known British firm and a BBC 'Nationwide' helicopter covered the Morecambe Bay test.

Although the trials seemed to go well in the Bay, it was apparently a different matter when the cart reached the Sahara where the fluctuations in wind strength are much greater. The cart had to be held firmly against the wind, but if this suddenly dropped it would then be over on its side. The wheels were found to be too narrow and, all in all, the going was extremely hard. The journey of two thousand miles took three months. Eventually, it was decided not to put the cart into production, but the prototype is preserved in store at the Science Museum, South Kensington.

A gaggle of geese

I suppose one of the most unusual requests came in July 2000 from Lucy Muller, a young woman farmer from Whitby. She wanted to raise money for a twelve-year old arthritis sufferer by walking with seventeen geese, starting on the west coast at Furness Abbey and crossing the Bay before continuing right across the country to finish at Whitby. She achieved her goal and I think the highlight of her journey must have been the Morecambe Bay section.

One of the most extraordinary crossings occurred in July 2000 when farmer Lucy Miller successfully achieved her goal of driving seventeen geese from Furness Abbey to Whitby – via Morecambe Bay! Here they are seen being gathered before setting out on the crossing.

Best feet forward in single file! Cedric is accompanied by his granddaughters Danielle Nickson (left) and Amy Robinson (right), with Lucy Miller driving the geese at the rear.

I took my two youngest granddaughters, Amy and Danielle, along with me as we set off at quite a pace with the geese close behind, making our way out into the open space of the Bay and on towards the River Kent crossing. Everything went well and we all came towards the end of this unusual crossing of the sands by finishing at White Creek, Arnside. I believe this was the next stopping place for the night. My job over for the day, we turned back the way we had come out and made our way back home.

'Keeper of the Kingdom'

In August 1997 Olive received a phone call from a Julian Calder, a London photographer who had just come from Buckingham Palace after speaking with the Queen and Prince Philip. If it was convenient for us, he would travel up to Grange-over-Sands by rail that very same day and hopefully get some good shots out in the Bay for a book by Alastair Bruce of Crionaich entitled, 'Keepers of the Kingdom'.

The weather was perfect and the evening light even better still. Julian Calder and I set out from Guide's Farm on my tractor at five-thirty in the evening and did not arrive back at the farm until nine. He then had to travel back to London by train. The picture chosen for the book was hung in the National Portrait Gallery in London for an exhibition. Olive and I received invitations to go to the preview but, unfortunately, we were unable to attend owing to other commitments.

Every month of the year

Jim Lowther from Preston came to be a regular figure out on the sands at weekends and we came to know each other so well as he hardly missed coming on a walk. Jim was a loner and would rather cross the sands on his own. Then he met up and made friends with Gordon Handslip, a retired grocer from Grange, who was born in 1893 and made his first crossing on in August 1955.

Gordon is the only person to have accompanied Jim Lowther across Morecambe Bay in every month of the year, but Jim told me that he had him worried at times. Gordon was nevertheless a remarkable man and when he was eighty-four he walked from Hest Bank to Grange in three hours ten minutes. His last crossing with Jim was in September 1980 when he was aged eighty-seven but he lived for another ten years until April 1990.

Jim, a friend for forty years, died in 2003 at the age of seventy-three. I had not seen him out in the Bay quite so frequently during the previous two or three years and did hear that he had not been too well. The Bay is not the kind of place you expect to meet up with someone unless you are on a guided walk or perhaps come across a lone fisherman from Flookburgh on his old tractor. I always looked forward to seeing Jim and having a chat, usually about the meandering River Kent that he had crossed so many times. He was so knowledgeable. On lots of occasions I would see him treading in the river catching flukes, the tasty flatfish he would take home for his tea. Jim was a very private person, who will be sadly missed by all who had the pleasure of being in his company.

Trousers down!

As my cross-Bay walks were about to start in April 2003, I received a phone call from Harry Brown at Torrisholme, near Morecambe. Olive knew him from years ago when his family lived in Ravenstown. Harry told me of a relative who was keen to do the walk but was very nervous of water, and had been so all her life. I told Harry to pass a message on to her saying that if she came along to make herself known to me, I would escort her personally through the river arm in arm. In fact, I would look after her.

She came and, just before crossing the Kent, as there was quite a strong breeze and the river was about knee high, I asked her if she would mind holding my stick and haversack while I rolled up my trousers. Everyone was now ready for the off and as I blew my whistle I put my arm around hers to make her feel secure. I kept asking her if she was all right and she replied "so far", and then when I looked at her she did look rather frightened. The river was a long way from one side to the other - about three hundred yards.

I said, "Don't look down at the river whatever, just set your eyes on the far bank and you will be alright." We came out of the river and I said to the lady, "Would you mind holding my stick and my bag while I pull my trousers down?" She was quick in replying, "I might have known you would want something in return".

I could not help laughing at what she had said and after the walk Harry rang us to tell us of how much his relative had enjoyed herself. Who knows, she may want to come again next year?

Morecambe Bay by night

One unforgettable experience is still talked about to this day. We had friends from Great Harwood, near Blackburn, staying with us at the farm for a week. As they were due to go home at the weekend and knowing that I had walks planned from Silverdale on the coming Saturday and Sunday, they asked if they could come along when I checked the sands and river crossing on the Friday. When I agreed, everyone was so pleased and now, as well as Gordon and his daughter Barbara, there would be my daughter Jean and a very young Terry Austerfield (a relative of ours from Leeds), Mark Holden (Jean's friend at the time) and me. Six of us altogether and they were all feeling excited about going across with one whom they called 'Uncle Ced'. We took the train from Kents Bank station to Silverdale on a most beautiful sunny afternoon in August 1981.

When we left home I gave Olive the approximate times when to look out for us and a rough idea of how long it would take us to cross if all went well. I got quite a surprise after leaving the shore at Silverdale to come across large areas of quicksands and mud in the same area that only two weeks ago I had led several hundred walkers across. I was disappointed and now had to make back to the shore and take the road to Jenny Brown's Point.

As we passed Gibraltar Farm the views across the Bay were spectacular with the setting sun by now quite low in the west but looking like a massive great orange. The daylight had almost gone and stars were appearing in the sky by the time we had walked down to the Point and out on to the sands to see if it was a suitable place to start the forthcoming walks. It was still pleasant enough but starting to get a little overcast.

It seemed an age from leaving Jenny Brown's point to coming near to the River Kent but I was content in my mind now that I could start the walks from the Point. At first my small entourage were quite full of themselves and there were lots of questions asked, but now, as visibility became poor, everyone went quiet and kept very close to me. I knew the Kent pretty well from my daytime visits to the area but there was only one safe place to cross and every stride we took now brought us nearer to the river. We could hear fast running water, which sounded like rapids.

It was frightening for my followers, as by now it was becoming dark and the stars had disappeared behind newly formed clouds. I had to reassure them that I knew exactly where we were and that the noise was coming from what is called a gullet. This is where a fairly wide river suddenly narrows creating a very fast flow known as a gillimer. I told them we would have to go much higher before attempting to cross the river as by now it was really dark. After walking for a while I estimated that we were far enough away from the gullet to attempt our crossing. I led the way into the river, wading slowly, stick in hand and testing the surface as I went forward, with five people very close behind me.

There was no way that we could see to the other side, as by now it was just too dark. The depth was just under knee and we had gone about 150 yards when suddenly there was this huge brack, like a wall about ten feet tall, immediately in front of us. The sand under our feet was becoming softer, so I shouted for them to turn round and go back the way we had come. When the sands firmed up again underfoot, I explained that with it being dark and us unable to see the course of the river, we had come higher up than we should have done. We slowly made our way down the river with the flow and, although this was pure guesswork with it being so dark, it brought us all together safely on the home stretch.

There were some sighs of relief. "By gum, Uncle Ced, that was frightening," came from young Terry. Gordon had a flashlight with him and thought he would keep shining it at intervals as we made our way towards Guide's Farm, leaving the eerie Kent well behind.

When we arrived back at the farm, Olive and Joan, Gordon's wife, had been worried sick. However, although we were a long way out of our estimated time, Olive knew that changes in the Bay can happen and things do not always go to plan. We all celebrated with a good meal and it was comforting just to sit there and listen to what they all had to say about this crossing of Morecambe Bay at night. Just a nightmare!

A load of hot air

During our forty years at the farm we have understandably met many people and made lots of new friends. On one of the most beautiful days in the summer of 1981 I arranged a walk from Hest Bank to Grange for the Cherry family, whom I had not previously met. The following March I received a letter from Peter, their 22-year old son, explaining that he wanted to write a book on Morecambe Bay and asking if it would it be possible to go out to the fishing grounds with me and take some photographs. Arrangements were duly made and Olive and I found that he was a very polite and well educated young man, rather shy at first, but he seemed to come out of his shell with more frequent visits to see us. After a while it was like coming home for him and we always made him welcome.

It was very good of the Cherry family to include us in some of Peter's birthday celebrations, when we were taken out to the Lakeside and Crooklands hotels and had wonderful meals. We did not always celebrate in such style, but many a time following a walk Olive and daughter Jean would prepare a superb buffet for us. If the weather was nice we could enjoy eating outdoors on the lawn with the wonderful views of the Bay.

One afternoon, in July 1987, the Cherry family had been on the Bay walk with me and were invited back to Guide's Farm for their tea. We were all sitting enjoying the relaxation and had just started our meal when suddenly we heard an almighty roar above our heads. It was a hot air balloon that was descending fast, just missing the chimney stack on the roof of Guide's Farm. They were so low that we shouted to the three occupants and we could see that they were going to come down very soon. As we watched, the huge balloon hit the dry sand almost tipping out its passengers, then it appeared to lift for a while but came down again about a mile from the shore.

These balloon enthusiasts always have a back-up vehicle to come to their aid, but on this unfortunate landing it was unable to travel across the sands to reach them as it got bogged down in soft sand not far out from the shore at Kents Bank. Luckily for them, they had been spotted by us at the farm and I wasted no time in going out to their rescue as the tide was coming in and was not too far from where they had landed.

The balloon canopy had already been rolled up in a tidy heap and there were just enough of us to lift the heavy basket onto the backboard of my tractor. The tide was only a matter of yards away from us as we drove slowly back towards Kents Bank station, where I helped transfer the heavy basket onto the back-up vehicle's trailer. The balloon belonged to Holker Estates and was valued at £10,000 so they were very pleased to see us all back.

The balloon trip that nearly ended in disaster had been intended as a sixty third birthday treat for Alfred Shepherd of Barrow. He believed they were going to crash as there was no wind to keep them up and as they came down they had, in fact, bounced three times on the sand before coming to a halt.

My good deed done for the day, I drove back to Guide's Farm to meet up with Olive, Jean, Chris and the Cherry family. I was able to finish my meal and discuss the rescue with them, although they had been able to watch what was happening quite clearly from the farm.

Last rites

Something totally different from anything I had been asked to do before was to carry out the wishes of three residents of Cart Lane. When they had died and been cremated, they wanted their ashes to be taken and scattered out in the Bay.

This I did on two occasions before the River Kent moved across to the other side of the Bay. Now it is just not the same, so with my most recent request I suggested that it would be better for me to travel round to Arnside and meet up with the family and their friends on the promenade. After these arrangements were settled, Olive and I set out from Grange with me looking smart and dressed like a funeral director. Olive did not take part in the service and sat patiently waiting in the car until it was all over.

I had earlier suggested what I thought would be the most suitable place, so after being introduced to the small party and having a brief chat, I asked them to follow me down onto the shore towards the edge of the Kent. Here we all stood solemnly and in silence. A member of the family was carrying a bunch of red roses and handed one to each of us, then took out a sheet of paper with some very nice wording that she read out.

The tide was just about to lap over our feet when I was given the urn containing the ashes. Now it was my turn. Nothing emerged with the first shake so I tried harder and you will rarely have seen what happened next. Well, if you pee into the wind you definitely get your own back! What had been a gentle breeze had become much stronger and I was covered in grey ash from head to toe - and so were some of the relatives. Nothing was said as we threw the roses onto the moving tide and then there was another reading from the sheet of paper

When it was all over and I returned to the car, Olive asked what I had been doing as my dark suit had changed colour to grey. I explained about the wind coming in with the tide as it does many a time, but some good came out of that day at Arnside. Olive now trims my hair and eyebrows almost weekly. She says she has never known anyone whose hair grows as quickly as mine does and, by the way, my suit had to go to the cleaners!

Birds of the Bay

Those crossing Morecambe Bay have much to see, especially if they are interested in birdlife. Swirling flocks of waders and wildfowl feed along the edge of the retreating tide. A closer look at these apparently barren and lifeless sandflats reveals the coil casts of thousands of lugworms on the surface. Birds burrow through the sand to feast on these worms and the tiny crustaceans and shellfish that lay hidden below the surface.

Some of the birds live in the Bay all year round, others migrate here in autumn and spring, and other flocks use it as an important feeding and rest stop, en route elsewhere. When you have seen the large flocks of knot and dunlin that swirl and swoop over the sands, it is easy to appreciate why Morecambe Bay has been designated a Ramsar site, which is a wetland of international importance, also a special protection area for birdlife.

Grasses, herbs and dwarf shrubs dominate mature salt marshes. A long history of sheep grazing has reduced the number of plant species that would otherwise occur in many parts of the Bay. Away from the nibbling sheep, different plants flourish such as the purple-flowered sea lavender and sea aster.

In winter, the marshes with their cropped grasses attract thousands of over-wintering wildfowl. Over two hundred thousand geese, swans, ducks, and wading birds arrive from Arctic Canada, Eastern Europe and Siberia. Many pink-footed geese use the Bay as a rest and refuelling stop on their lonely migrations to and from the Arctic and several thousand of these are enticed to stay and over-winter around the Lune estuary and here on the salt marshes at Grange-over-Sands and Kents Bank.

The sheer scale of Morecambe Bay can accommodate these enormous flocks of waders and wildfowl and the abundance of its food supply can support them. As the tide ebbs, this allows the birds to feast on juicy worms, shellfish, shrimps, crabs and the like.

The fringes of the salt marshes, shingle banks and tidally exposed scars provide secure roosts at night, with over thirty thousand oystercatchers and three thousand curlew who gather at a winter roost near the Kent Estuary. Their distinctive piping and bubbling calls carry across the Bay. Over-wintering eider ducks are attracted by the quantity of small mussels, their favourite food, and often several hundred gather off Walney. their most southerly breeding colony on the west coast of Britain. Islands are vital havens for breeding birds. Walney Island has one of the largest gull colonies in Europe. Terns rest in large noisy colonies on the shingle ridges of Walney and Foulney and can be seen plunging into the sea to catch whitebait and sand eels.

Morecambe Bay is a unique place, but designations for quantities and qualities of habitat and birdlife are not the only things that make it special. A number of factors, much harder to define and measure, combine to create the landscape of the Bay. The unique views of the Lakeland fells, the vast expanse of the tidal sandflats, the tranquillity, the shifting sands, the light and the sense of history and heritage, all make the Bay a very special place to the many people who live there or visit the area.

DUNLIN.

CORMORANT.

COMMON SHELD-DUCK.

STORM PETREL

G. Robinson.

OYSTER CATCHER.

LESSER BLACK-BACK GULL.

Part 2
Portrait of
Morecambe Bay

A pictorial look at the unique part of Britain's coast that has variously been described as 'a wet Sahara' and 'a great inner sea'. There can be no doubting its ever changing light and infinite variety.

Between the tides. The wonderful effect of sunshine on the numerous pools left behind by the retreating sea.

Panorama towards the Lakeland fells from Arnside with Kent viaduct striding across the Bay in the middle distance.

Boat on the Arnside shore.

Out in the middle of the Bay near the fluke nets.

Samphire, known locally as Poor Man's Asparagus, grows on many parts of the shore. Cedric and Olive eat this tasty plant.

The Bay looking more like the dry rather than the wet Sahara. This scene, taken in hot summer weather, looks out from the marsh at Kents Bank towards Morecambe.

Remnants of the old pier at Hest Bank, which has recently emerged from the sands after being lost from view for around a century.

Footprints galore, left behind by dozens of walkers striding across the sands.

Sea shells on the sea shore – one of the many facets of the Bay that is easily overlooked.

Tracks in the sand – created by the Sandpiper.

The shoreline is ever changing as dramatically seen here at Flookburgh.

The wild side of Morecambe Bay, viewed from near Flookburgh with sea protection works on the bottom left of the photograph.

Those close to the Bay never tire of its magnificent sunsets.

Cedric at the fluke nets – a photograph taken at the time of a television documentary 'Men of the Wet Sahara', which covered fishing activities in the Bay.

Flookburgh Fishermen and their Nicknames

Real name	Nickname	Real name	Nickname
William Holborn Robinson (my father)	Alderman	Johnty Butler	Clarty
		Frank Benson	Giah
Maurice Robinson (his brother)	Homey	Harold Couperthwaite	Whiskers
		Jim Benson	Lion
Jim Robinson (his older brother)	Carey		(later Sir James)
		Frank Dickinson	Moke
		Edward Benson	Ned
The three Butler brothers:		Jim Burrow	Naylor
Harold Butler	Taro	Tom Wilson	Old Tom
Bill Butler	Pongo	William Couperthwaite	Will
John Butler	Me-fat	Jim Butler	Shiggar
		Jim Butler	Ganza
McClure	Fishy	Robert Butler	Carrots (red head)
Harold Manning	Hunter	Jack Stephenson	Chippy Jack

Part 3
Fishing and Fisherfolk

Following the Sands

From Rampside, at the entrance of the Walney channel, the coast road turns to the north-west and forms low ground to Newbiggin. A little further along the coast lies Aldingham, a village five miles east of Barrow-in-Furness and four miles south of Ulverston. Legend has it that part of the village, close to the church, was engulfed by sand and sea. From here the land rises very steeply from the shoreline to the village of Baycliff.

Along this stretch of coastline, fishing families have followed the sands for their livelihood for centuries. There is no doubt they were a hardy breed. At one time all the established fishing families had deeds for the area where they fished, and each family would jealously guard their own territory.

There were many familiar characters along this stretch of coastline and one of them was old Maggie Coward from the village of Scales. She would be seen with her horse and cart going out onto the sands to set nets for plaice and she also gathered cockles which she took to her customers in Barrow-in-Furness. She was a widow and this was her way of making a living.

As a young lad leaving school and starting to follow the sands as a fisherman, I certainly found Flookburgh to be a village, full of characters in their own right. Most of them had nicknames as shown in the accompanying list. Dad told me that he went shrimping with Pincha, Johnny Wright and Bill Hartley, a Silverdale fisherman who took the nickname of Eggy. My predecessor, Bill Burrow of Cart Lane, had the nickname of Whapper. However did they come to be given these names in the first place? They were all interesting characters and now they have all gone. I have some very happy memories, which live on, as I knew all but one of the names listed here.

Generations of Flookburgh families, together with other fishermen from surrounding villages, have earned their living from the sea and sands of Morecambe Bay. For many of the families working in the Bay, including our own, cockle fishing was the main source of our livelihood and there were hard times after the harsh winter frost of 1962-3. This decimated the cockle stocks and they did not begin to recover until the 1970s.

When I started to follow the sands with my dad the most important job in the cold winter months was gathering cockles for the market towns of Lancashire and Yorkshire. Although cockles can be gathered all the year round, it was impossible to transport them during the summer as they would not keep as fresh as in the cool of winter. We did not have the luxury of refrigerators and freezers in those days! But whatever the weather, wind or rain or even fog, we would set out on the long journey into the Bay to fulfil our orders and try to make a living.

Our methods used were unique to the area and very unusual to people from elsewhere. Fishing is usually done from a boat but that is not possible from Flookburgh. The tide goes out for many miles, leaving sandbanks high and dry, with dykes and gullies which have been given names by the fishermen over the years. These drain down the sands back to the main rivers, which are the Kent and the Leven. We used horses and carts to take us out so, as well as learning about the sands from my father, I also had to be able to look after the horse. Our lives depended upon a good and reliable horse!

Following the sands is a dangerous occupation and even with a lifetime's experience one is never too old to learn. One gets used to living with these dangers and over the years tends to get wiser. A well-known saying is 'a little knowledge is a dangerous thing'. However, when someone has a lifetime's experience on the sands and is a steady and level-headed person who can be trusted and followed, one can say that 'knowledge dispels fear'.

When still a very young lad I was eager to learn and start fishing alongside my father with my very own horse and cart. In 1947 I left school behind at the age of fourteen and never felt happier. Most of my school pals left to go into a trade such as joinery, building or plumbing but I just wanted to follow the sands. In the winter months I went with my father gathering the cockles and had to work really hard to keep warm out on the sands but, as spring arrived and the weather improved, with the days growing lighter, we would each take a horse and cart.

Dad would stop off at the cockle beds about three or four miles out in the heart of the Bay and I would continue another mile or so down to the shrimping grounds. When dad was asked how his lad was doing at fishing he replied that he was shaping well. He admits that he was always a bit worried about me shrimping down the Bay on my own and felt a sigh of relief when he spotted me on the horizon, coming up from the lower grounds to meet up with him once again.

I have fished the Bay all of my life for cockles, shrimps, mussels, flukes and whitebait. Shrimping went on from March till the first signs of frosts, usually about October into November, and if these were severe for a few nights in succession it brought the season to an abrupt end. Olive was good at shelling shrimps – locally known as 'picking' – as were all members of our family. There were other very good pickers in Ravenstown and Cark as well as Flookburgh so some of the shrimps were sent out to various households in buckets and then collected later the same day.

Shelling shrimps, known locally as 'picking', has long been a way of life for the Robinson family, all of whom are considered to be good 'pickers'. Olive, daughter Jean, John Shaw and Cedric are busy at work at Guide's Farm in about 1981.

A group of walkers watch Cedric demonstrate how to set a Bawk Net. This method of fishing is now obsolete and has been superseded by the easier Trap Net.

Prices were often poor with very little return for all the hard work put in by the fishermen. The outlets for our fish - mainly cockles and shrimps - were the markets in the Lancashire and Yorkshire towns. Fishermen were getting more and more disheartened and began to think that they were being conned out of their payment, as 'condemned' notes came through their letter boxes from the wholesale fishmongers with increasing frequency. At that time there were about twenty-five fishermen in Flookburgh working the Bay from horses and carts. My father once told me that when he left school and started fishing with his father and his mother, there must have been at least one hundred fishermen and women with cockling and musseling being the main industry. There was no dole money in those days so they had to go fishing irrespective of whether they caught 'owt or nowt', because that was the only thing to do.

I often think back to those days and was especially interested to come across the following description of what fishing was like even earlier around a hundred years ago.

Fishermen of Old

An account of the Flookburgh cockle fishermen and their contemporaries, written almost a century ago superbly captures the atmosphere of those days.

I learned in the village that the tide was coming in and the cocklers are always ahead of it, so I walked down the long white road to meet them. The tang of the sea was in my nostrils. A great silence lay over the vast stretches of country which rolled away to the front of Coniston Old Man and the hills of the Lake District, twenty miles behind me. There was not a human being in sight, but still I walked towards the sea, for the approaching cocklers were doubtless hidden in the faint mist that hung over the Bay.

I had hardly reached the end of the road when I heard the sound of a creaking cart and voices in the distance. And soon, right away across the vast expanse of sand, two tiny dots came into view and gradually, as the minutes went by, each increased in size until I could make out two horse drawn carts, each with a driver perched on the front. Both carts had a number of sacks in the bottom, which I presumed were full of cockles. There were also a number of baskets among the load and a queer wooden instrument that was like a plant, about three feet long, out of which jutted two handles.

A few moments later I was talking to Tom Wilson – Flookburgh's crack cockler. I learned afterwards. He told me that the instrument was a 'jumbo' and was placed upon the sand and pulled gently to and fro by the handles. This causes the sand to become watery and the cockles beneath to rise to the surface.

He said that they had been five miles out across the sands, as the cockles were better out there. He and his comrades left home at three o'clock that morning and were only just returning. It was then about half past eleven. Tom was in a hurry to get his cockles to the railway station, so when he arrived back at the little grey village he introduced me to Jim Burrow, a jovial, red faced little man who roared with laughter on the slightest provocation.

On a bank the cocklers are in a dangerous position, and all the time are working against the clock, for if they are tempted by good cockle grounds to stay just a minute or two longer than is really safe, they will find themselves surrounded by water. If the horse is a good one, it will take to the water without hesitation and make a valiant effort to reach safety. Cocklers' horses have been known to swim through deep water channels, dragging the floating cart and all its load behind.

Then there is the perilous fog which sometimes descends upon these hardy folk. In such time, only a cool head will retain its sense of direction, Jim told me, and a steady hand and discerning eye guide the horse and its load through the shifting quicksands to firm ground again.

"You know Tom Wilson, who introduced you to me?" said Jim, and I nodded. "Well he's the best cockler we've had in this country for years. He is as good as any two men. And not afraid to go out by himself. Not many men will go cockling without a mate – but Tom will. Aye, he's a good lad is Tom. A lot of other young fellows round here are drifting into other jobs. The demand for cockling is not so great as it was. Too much competition from places like Lytham, who can run their fish into the big towns in their motor vehicles in a few minutes. But Lytham cockles are not a patch on ours."

Flookburgh fisherfolk at work over a century ago – a photograph that superbly captures the traditional method of cockling described in this account. A horse and a cart containing hay and some oats were taken out into the Bay. The cart was then tipped on its end, thus keeping the fodder dry and enabling it to be reached by the horse, which was covered with a rug to keep it warm. Cockling now began in earnest. The figure on the left is using a 'jumbo', a thick plank of wood with primitive handles, which was rocked to and fro on the wet sand until the cockles showed on the surface. The woman on the right is following with a 'cramb', a curved fork with metal handles used to spear the cockles and put them in baskets. When these were full the contents were tipped into large hessian sacks, which can be seen attached to the back of the cart, and the catch was finally taken ashore.

As we were talking, up came eighty two year old Will Hutton, who deliberated long and hard on the enormous difference between Lytham and Flookburgh cockles. "Why at Lytham." he cried, "They get 'em a few yards out – little black cockles that's no good to anybody. Thousands of 'em there are and they just spade 'em up. Spade 'em up!" he shouted, throwing his hands up in indignation. "Then there's these 'ere scared about cockles. Well you can tell 'em from me, I've been catching' 'em and eating 'em all my life, and there's nowt ails me – nowt!"

In high dudgeon, Old Will stumped off down the white road towards the sea, with a little sack over his shoulder. "Old Will can't keep away from yon sands," said Jim, "He's worked night and day on 'em, in all weathers, since he was a bit of a lad."

Then, Dick Burrow, a relative of Jim's, strolled across to us. Dick is a bachelor and lives by himself and has finished taking any active part in cockling. He confessed to me has was getting a little too old for it, and the demand for the fish did not warrant the effort.

Dick told of the laws governing the use of the 'jumbo'. The Fishermen's Board have ruled that these contraptions must be used only for four months during the winter. In the summer, a three-pronged hand tool (cramb) made by the local blacksmith is employed to flick the cockles out of the sand, which means slow work. The object of this bye-law is to prevent the flooding of the markets. So Dick says. A riddle must also be used so that no undersized cockles are sent to the market.

"Often," said Dick, "the inspectors of the Fisheries Board would lie in wait on the white road and examine the loads in the carts to see that the cockles were all well up to size, and during the summer months to see that no 'jumbo' was being carried. Why before the bye-laws about jumboes, we used to make 'em up to twenty seven feet long. Now we are only allowed to make 'em three feet long."

And he added, "It takes a good eye to see the cockles." And as he spoke, a great flock of birds swept overhead. "We can get three pence apiece for them birds," said Dick. "Oystercatchers, black and white, we call 'em sea-a-pies, with long orange beak and legs. They can live up to twenty-five year of age and can take as many cockles a day as the fishermen. We catch 'em wi' nets. Not bad eating either, as long as you soak 'em in water before roasting!"

Then up came Will Wright, another cockle man, with Ned, and Will told me of a hair-raising escape he once had from being trapped by the tide. "We set out about three o'clock in the morning," he said, "and made a direct line for Barrow Lighthouse, which shines right across the sands in clear weather. The cockling was good. We struck good beds of cockles, but the tide came in sooner than we had expected. We had to get the horses to gallop for it.

"T'horse was up to his knees in water, but we were going well, and I thought we were to get through alright when suddenly he fell into a hole as deep as its back. But my horse is no duffer, an' 'e swam. Lucky for me that t'cart was flat bottomed and floated fairly well. We got into t'shallows again and galloped, but again, we got into a hole. And so it went on, shallows, and then a hole, but each time the shallow water was getting deeper and deeper. We was lucky to get out that time – by gum we was!"

And all the three old men, and Ned, who was younger, began to talk and laugh boisterously, treating narrow escapes from death as a joke. They talked of good cockling, and bad cockling, deplored the gradual decline of the industry, and the number of young men taking mechanics, overalls and farm labourers in clogs. Soon, they thought, the familiar blue jersey and long sea boots would soon be seen no more in Flookburgh. They had already disappeared from Cark, the next village.

I talked to Mrs Hill, the confectioner, and she gave me one or two recipes for the preparing of cockles. Firstly, soak the cockles, preferably overnight, in a bucket of cold water, with a handful of oatmeal added. This helps to clean them. Then boil them and take them from the shells. Serve in a dish after adding salt and vinegar. Eat with brown bread and butter.

The afternoon was warming when I came out of Mrs Hill's shop and the village appeared to be sleeping. I walked down the long white road again and sat on a piece of driftwood at the bottom of the marsh and watched the blood red sun sink over this great strip of sea, then sink over the Barrow promontory. A cheerful glow could now be seen from the windows of the cottages and farms dotted here and there on the distant hillsides. The lapping of the receding water died away and soon, even the birds hushed their complaints.

There was a rumble on the white road and, after a few minutes, a cockle cart sank from the gravel into the soft sand and ploughed silently on and away through the crimson path of the sun's reflections; very soon fading to a speck among the rolling banks of sand. Old Tom, as he was called by the villagers, followed the sands all his life, and kept going right up until the age of ninety years. His daughter Ethel told me this excellent true story with a fisherman's flavour to it.

"Dad would come home from the sands with his catch of cockles and always washed a basket full extra clean, which were put outside the front door for sale to the locals, along with the quart measure." Ethel said to her Dad, "Now Dad, you'll be ready for something to eat."

"Aye," he said, "I is, but ah 'moant' sit eer long, cos-av-oor much ta doo, 'av ardly time to bree-ath this morning."

Ethel said to herself, good gracious me, nearly ninety and hasn't time to breathe. Anyway, a knock came on the door and Ethel opened it and this very smart gentleman was stood there – he raised his hat and said "good morning" in a high pitched very posh voice. Ethel said good morning to him.

"How ma-a-rch are your cockles?" he asked, just like that. But before Ethel had the chance to answer the man, her dad shouted from the back kitchen. "Fower - punce - a qu-a-a-rt."

The posh man said "Oh right, I'll have a qu-a-a-rt then." Poor Ethel couldn't measure them for laughing. So, of course, when Ethel had got his qu-a-a-rt measured into a bag, the man looked at them and said, "I think I will have another qu-a-a-rt as they look so nice."

And her Dad shouted again, "Aye - therr - oh - reet, thev just cumt off this morning, but yah moh-nt boil em oor lang." As the man left, he raised his hat and said good morning. When Ethel came back into the house, her dad said. "Ew wha-a-s that fello'h then?"

Ethel said she didn't know him and thought him to be a stranger, but didn't know what he would make of what her dad had said to him in what must have seemed some foreign language, but this was the local dialect spoken by all the Flookburgh fishermen in those days.

Ethel said, "Why didn't you say four pence a quart, dad? Instead of fower - punce - a - qu-a-a-rt." and he said, "well he called it a qu-a-a-rt didn't he, he's nah better than me!"

Well these fisher folk were hardy characters, born and bred, probably never to be equalled again.

Cockles to Market

There is nothing nice about cockling in high winds that dry out the sands and make it difficult to use the jumbo board on the cockle beds. Our equipment had to be looked after out there with no shelter at all. I was shown as a lad that there was a right and wrong way to set the cockle basket and the riddle down on the sands without the strong wind sending them reeling for miles at such a speed you could never recover them.

When cockle beds are plentiful a combination of high tides and winds can move them quite long distances. They are usually brought to a halt by a build-up of sand or a dyke. When we found such cockles they were a welcome sight as they could usually be gathered without needing to use the jumbo.

When our daughter Jean left school she followed the sands with me cockling, mostly through the winter months for the markets of Blackburn and Burnley. There were any amount of good quality cockles in Morecambe Bay but orders for them were few and far between as our markets were being flooded with imports from Holland at such low prices that it made it difficult to compete and make a living.

As Jean and I worked out on the sands cockling during the daytime, we would travel at night to arrive at the wholesalers about 3.30am. We always took a flask of coffee and a blanket with us as it became very cold sitting in the car if we arrived much earlier than anticipated and had to wait until they opened.

Our cockles were transported in a trailer towed behind my car. On one occasion we were driving along towards Blackburn after leaving the M6 motorway and thinking how good it was travelling through the night as we met so little traffic. Out of the blue the lights of a car showed in my mirror. As it approached the driver pulled alongside us, keeping parallel for quite a distance with the passenger glaring at me. I said to Jean, "What are those silly so-and-so's up to?" Then suddenly they sped off in front of us and a sign lit up their rear window reading 'Police - Stop'. We did and the two plain clothes men came to my driver's side as I opened the window. They asked me lots of questions, seemed satisfied that we were genuine and left us to continue our journey.

It was not always pleasant travelling at night as I can recall on our return journey home from Blackburn market to Grange. The rains came down like never before and we could hardly see the road in front of us. I did not have fixed rear lights on the car trailer so I had concocted some. A wooden pole fixed horizontally across the back with two bicycle rear lamps on either side looked pretty good when we set out from Grange. As we approached Forton Services on our return journey, the vibration on the way there must have loosened the rear lamps and they were now facing downwards with batteries running low!

A police patrol vehicle pulled us over with his bright flashing lights dazzling us in the horrible misty rain. The policeman was on his own and came towards us, then walked round to the back of our trailer. He came forward to me and said, "Do you know that you have no rear lights on your trailer?" Then he asked me to step out of the car and take a look for myself.

He asked me lots of questions including details of where we lived. When I told him Grange-over-Sands and that I was born in Flookburgh he became interested and told me that he had friends there and gave me their names. I knew them well so now instead of 'going by the book' he advised

Jean and Cedric demonstrate the traditional method of cockling to a visiting film crew.

me to pull into Forton Services and spend time there until it became daylight instead of continuing our journey home and probably getting into more trouble. You can sometimes read a person by looking at them and this policeman had a good face and temperament to go with it. Jean and I thought that we had been very lucky as we sat over our cups of tea and looked across to a table. Chatting over a cuppa not far away from where we were sitting was a group of policemen, including the one whom had stopped us earlier.

The last time I delivered cockles to Blackburn market I vowed that I would never ever do so again by road. I was driving a van loaded with six hundredweight of cockles when it broke down close to the Blackburn turn-off from the M6. I managed to slip onto the hard shoulder just before the River Ribble. I saw lights across the fields so I left the old van and was frightened to death while crossing over the river as there was no hard shoulder and traffic was so close to me. I arrived at the Tickled Trout Hotel in the middle of the night and must have looked like a tramp. I had been cockling during the daytime, had not shaven and was wearing a long dark coat and my waders. A very polite young lady eventually appeared at the desk after I had been ringing the bell for some time.

I told her who I was, explained my predicament and asked if I could possibly use their phone. She not only allowed me to do so but also looked through the phone directory and then got through to my friend, Larry Bennett, a builder in Grange. I thanked her and made my way back towards the motorway, hoping that Larry would work something out. It was so cold and frosty that night as I sat in the van unable to keep warm. Suddenly, the police arrived and gave me a good telling off, saying that I could not leave the vehicle there on the motorway and asking what arrangements I had made to have it removed. I told them that a friend was on his way to help me so they left me in peace.

It did not seem too long before Larry pulled onto the hard shoulder just behind me.   He had brought along a large flask of coffee and we were just drinking the stuff (or was it nectar?) when another police car arrived and out jumped two of them. We explained what had happened and fortunately they were quite sociable.

Larry had just purchased a brand new Rover car and after we had drunk the coffee he put the seats down, spread out a cover and loaded the six hundredweight of cockles. Just imagine - how many people would subject their new car to this treatment? Larry attached a rope to the old van and towed it to a lay-by, where we unhitched it and drove on to Blackburn to deliver the cockles. On our return I jumped back into the van and Larry towed me all the way back to Grange. I shall never forget that night and what Larry and Christine, his wife, did for me. They are both truly remarkable friends.

Searching for Starfish

A type of fishing that was totally new to me and probably to Morecambe Bay was to gather starfish from the mussel scars not very far out from Heysham village. The starfish, which were about the size of a hand, had come in with the tide in their thousands and settled on the scars to feed on the mussels. The late John Foster of Grange asked if I would be interested in having a go at gathering them in for him. He told me that he had been onto the scars to have a look and thought it would be safe enough to work on them with my tractor.

I knew from earlier experience that this was not the case and to take a tractor on to the mussel scars would be asking for trouble. The sand on and around them may appear hard enough to the layperson but it contains a lot of clay. I needed the tractor to transport the starfish but left it a safe distance away. I then used a wheelbarrow to carry the fish-boxes and trays holding the starfish after they had been plucked from the mussel beds. I say 'plucked' because you could not just pick them up. They were under water, usually about knee deep, and had attached themselves to the mussels with a suction pad.

Picking starfish from the mussel beds made our hands very sore, as it was like handling sandpaper the whole of the time, so we decided to wear rubber gloves and these worked a treat. There was not a lot of time between tides to work on these beds, low down in the Bay, so it was essential to start collecting the starfish as soon as we knew the water had gone off the scars. We needed footwear for protection from the sharp mussel shells, with trousers and sleeves rolled up as far as we could get them, and then we would start 'plucking'. My son-in-law Chris worked on the scars with me until the starfish became hard to find.

While doing this work I noticed that an island appeared way out in the distance on the extreme tides, so I mentioned this to Larry Bennett, our good friend. Larry just loved a challenge and as Chris had already told him of the island, he suggested right away that he would come along with his four-wheel drive pick-up and with his small boat secured on a trailer to do a recce.

I went along with Larry and Chris the very next day as we drove around the Bay, through Morecambe and down to the little village of Heysham. From the square we took the narrow road down past several shops and the ancient St Patrick's Chapel on the left and out into the Bay. The sands journey from here was only a matter of minutes and when we arrived at a safe place to stop the three of us took the boat from the trailer and carried it to the water's edge. From here on I wanted nothing more to do with this expedition! Larry and Chris jumped into the flimsy small boat, put the oars in place and away they went out into the distance, with only a few inches showing above the water line. I stayed with Larry's vehicle and hoped for the best and their safe return.

They were quite pleased with themselves when they got back but not as pleased as I was to see them return safely. If the wind had struck up with the incoming tide, as it does many a time, they may just have been in trouble. The following day they left Grange in high spirits as they had found lots of starfish and were now on their way to sail out to the island in the sun. I was not happy about this as to sail all that way and put extra weight in that flimsy little boat was taking a big risk. They got simply loads of starfish and went back and forth sailing to the island over several days, but then the tides changed and it was covered with water until the next extreme tides.

The starfish were brought back to Guide's Farm where they were first washed and then stood in containers filled with fresh water to allow them to set in their natural shape. They were later taken out of the water and put into buckets containing formalin, then tightly sealed and sent to American universities for research purposes. Fishing for starfish was a very short season but it was different - and we three did enjoy ourselves out there in the Bay!

All Sorts of Fish

Has global warming arrived? It is a question everyone is asking and especially the fishermen of Morecambe Bay. There is no doubt that recent weather patterns in the United Kingdom have had everyone talking about global warming and the impact of climate change. It has been suggested that there will be an increase in rainfall, but it will occur in shorter and heavier deluge conditions. The end result could be hotter summers, wetter winters and terrible storms. In hotter summers the land is baked and cannot take these heavy downpours. So when this happens the rainfall is taken away almost immediately, like water off a duck's back, and runs down to the nearest rivers and streams and from then on it flows into the estuaries. This, in time, adds to rising sea levels.

We seem to have lost our four seasons. Gone are the hard winters I knew as a child when almost every family in the village of Flookburgh owned a sledge and the snow seemed to lie for ages. Even though it was bitterly cold, everyone enjoyed sledging. One severe winter of frosts in 1981-82 killed off most of the cockle beds in Morecambe Bay and made it hard for the fishermen to scrape a living.

Until forty years ago porpoise were seen in large numbers coming up the Bay with the tide. They were wonderful to watch, appearing out of the water and diving under again. Salmon were plentiful at the time and that would be why the porpoises came up the Bay. Seals used to surface on the rocks close to Cart Lane and they too were a delight to watch. Ned Benson, a Flookburgh fisherman, once caught one in his fluke nets and brought it ashore before putting it on display for the village folk in a large bathtub of water.

It is now common practice for the Flookburgh and Morecambe fishermen to catch plaice, sole,

Fish of many kinds are now to be found in the Bay. These two boys are proudly holding a large dogfish, while the boy on the right also has a flounder in his hand.

skate, sea bass and codling, some in stake nets and others in the trawl net. These fishermen work much lower down in the Bay nearer to the deeper waters. This is good news because the last time I caught codling in the Bay was almost forty years ago. This was late in the season in stream nets near the River Leven and in such large catches we almost filled the cart. But as soon as the severe frosts came we didn't catch another fish that season.

Very rarely, large fish such as whales and dolphins are seen in the estuaries. According to the coastguard, a whale was stranded off the west coast of Cumbria in 1948. In September 1980, a twenty three foot whale was washed up on the shore at Sunderland Point. Tourists and locals alike caused a traffic build up as they flocked to see the giant mammal. It was decided to cut up the carcass as it would have been no easy task transporting a three-ton whale. The bone inside the mouth, which is used to filter food, was sent to the Natural History Museum in London for identification and the skeleton to Lancaster University. It was another four or five years before anyone could see the complete skeleton. Other large whales have been stranded more recently. They live in deeper water and travel in small groups, but one must get separated from the others. When they enter shallow water and areas like Morecambe Bay, they must panic and run themselves ashore.

A large dolphin was recently seen well up the estuary at Arnside. Although the coastguards were alerted at night and went to its assistance, there was little that could be done. On the next tide it was able to swim, but sadly it swam the wrong way and was stranded again. When it was first found by the coastguards, they told me that they thought it wasn't too well. It had a cut near its mouth, so a vet was called to give it an injection just before the tide arrived. When the tidal bore came they watched and thought it would now be able to swim back the way it came, but unfortunately this didn't happen. It ran aground much further up the estuary and there was nowhere for it to go. Eventually, it was decided that it had to be destroyed and the carcass taken away to be buried.

According to the experts, the sight of the world's second largest mammal cruising through the waters off the coast of Cumbria is set to become more common due to an increase in sea temperatures. Fin whale have begun to venture closer to the coast of Britain and can now be spotted from several points along the north-west coast such as Silverdale, Morecambe, Workington, Heysham and Maryport. They can reach a maximum length of eighty eight feet and they need to surface every six to ten minutes to blow. I wouldn't like to think of one of those lying in my fishing nets when I arrived at them in the dark!

More on the fishing industry, the history and ecology of Morecambe Bay and historic images from the collections at Lancaster Maritime and Fleetwood museums can be found on: www.nettingthebay.org.uk

Part 4

Death on the Sands

An Early Tragedy

On his 1769 visit, the poet Thomas Gray crossed the River Lune near Lancaster and walked the three miles to the village of Poulton (now Morecambe). He recorded in his Journal:

An old fisherman minding his nets (while I enquired about the danger of passing these sands) told me in his dialect a moving story. How a brother of the trade, a cockler as he styled him, driving a little horse-drawn cart with two daughters (grown women) in it, and his wife following on horseback, set out one day to cross the seven mile sands, as they had been frequently used to doing; for nobody in the village knew them better than the old man did.

When they were about half way over a thick fog rose, and as they drove on they found water much deeper than they expected. The old man was puzzled; he stopped and said he would go a little way to find some mark he was acquainted with. They stood a while for him; in vain they called aloud, but no reply came. At last the young women pressed their mother to think where they were and to go on. They wandered about forlorn and amazed. The mother would not quit her horse and get into the cart with her daughters. They determined, after much time was wasted, to turn back and give themselves up to the guidance of the horses.

The mother was soon washed off her horse and perished. The poor girls clung close to their cart and the horse, sometimes wading and sometimes swimming, brought them back to land alive, but senseless with terror and distress and unable for many days to give any account of themselves. The bodies of their parents were found the next ebb, that of the father a very few paces distant from the spot where he had left them.

Tragedies of Tudor Times

Deaths in Morecambe Bay recorded in Cartmel Parish Register:

1576	12th September. One young man drowned in the broadwater of Morecambe Bay.
1577	24th September. One little man, round faced, which was drowned at Grange.
1578	19th-20th September. George Mackereth drowned upon Kent Sands.
1597	9th September. Henry Inglish being drowned on Furness Sands.
1598	22nd October. Richard Beeslaye being drowned upon Kent Sands.
1603	25th July. John Parke, son of John of the parish of Dalton, was drowned upon Kent Sands.
1606	28th February. Elizabeth the wife of George Riggpin was drowned upon the sands near to Raven Winder Farm.
1606	3rd December. Anne Hawkes of Warton drowned on Carmel Sands.

Disasters in the Nineteenth Century

In 1803 Thomas Warbrick of Halton Foundry, near Lancaster, found his partner drowned as his gig had missed the fording place in the river. In 1811 the regular cross-Bay coach was caught in a blizzard. The driver, John Fowler, evacuated the passengers to safety and then went back to release the horses but was never seen again.

The Kent and Keer are fickle and seldom crossed light-heartedly. Danger is always lurking and ready to trap the unwary. In 1814, chaise drivers Dawson and Dobson were overtaken by the tide and drowned whilst returning from Holker Hall to Lancaster with four horses, one of which was also drowned.

It was some three years later when the first mail coach took to crossing the sands. In 1821 the 'Westmorland Flower', a Royal Mail coach, became stuck in the sands. The driver had to complete the journey on foot. One man drowned but another managed to free the coach by using beer barrels tied to the side. When the tide came in, it floated the coach out! I can imagine the poor soul sat on top clinging for dear life as the tide rolled past. There is no mention of what happened to the man and, come to think about it, what was a mail coach doing carrying beer?

In 1825 high winds blew the Ulverston mail coach over and one horse was drowned, but with the help of the passengers, the vehicle was righted and able to continue its journey. From about 1834 coach travel across Morecambe Bay ceased to operate for a period of some fifteen years, owing to it becoming increasingly dangerous. Crossings resumed when the sands and rivers were once again accessible.

Two of the worst disasters on the Bay happened with a total loss of twenty-one lives and an interval of eleven years, connected by one and the same fisherman's cart. On June 4th 1846, nine young people aged between seventeen and twenty-five drowned while crossing the Leven sands between ten and eleven o'clock at night. They had been to the Whitsuntide fair at Ulverston, where Thomas Moore of Flookburgh, owner of the cart, and Ellen Inman bought wedding clothes on the eve of their marriage.

Other people were crossing the sands at the time and said they saw the cart ford the River Leven near to the notorious Black Scars but then it suddenly disappeared. Any cries for help must have been lost on the wind. One man following on behind found all the young men and women and the horse drowned in a large hole, thought to have been caused by a coastal vessel unloading there on the previous tide. When the dead were laid to rest in Cartmel churchyard the following Sunday at 2pm, the church bells began to ring muffled peels and continued at intervals until 6pm before the last coffin was lowered into the grave. A crowd of almost 1,500 people attended the service.

Following that tragic fatality, the Moore family sold the cart to a Flookburgh fisherman named Benson and, in 1857, it was loaned to twelve young men who wanted to go to the Lancaster Fair. At the time, the River Keer ran close into Priest Skeer, a rocky outcrop about half a mile out in the Bay from Bolton-le-Sands. Here also was hidden danger as horse and cart plunged out of their depth and all twelve men and the horse were drowned. There runs a local saying of the moving quicksands: 'The Kent and Keer have parted many a good man and his mare.' The bodies were later recovered and taken to Herring House at Morecambe to be identified. The Bay usually gives up its dead.

Today's walkers gathering at Arnside are left in no doubt of the dangers of Morecambe Bay. Prominent in the background is Kent viaduct, which radically changed the nature of the estuary when it was completed. Opening of the railway in 1857 also massively reduced the amount of traffic across the Bay, although it did not prevent a tragedy in the same year when twelve young men were drowned.

Four years earlier in 1853 the first church at Grange-over-Sands was completed. The Reverend Rigg, the first vicar, almost lost his life in the over-sands coach when travelling from Manchester with the title deeds to take up his duties. The coach sank in the quicksands and was rapidly going down. The leather traces were cut and the passengers had got safely out of the sinking vehicle, when the coachman suddenly remembered there was someone inside. The old gentleman was entirely oblivious of much that was happening and, being a person in very delicate health, had shut all the windows and muffled himself with many layers of rugs. He was only released with much difficulty through the window, the doors already being deep in the sand. Months later the coach was finally washed up beside Holme Island, near to Grange, having been sucked out of the sands then rolled by the tide for a distance of four or five miles. The Rev Rigg's valise was recovered from the coach with the deeds and parchments still intact. They were scarcely legible, but sufficient to prove his rights of ownership.

Crossing the sands was a dangerous and difficult operation, but this did not deter the many travellers who used the route regularly. Cartmel Parish registers show many entries of people drowned while attempting the treacherous crossing. From the late sixteenth century until 1880 such burial entries number no less than one hundred and forty one.

Fishing Fatalities

An old fisherman from Bolton-le-Sands, who was known to be a loner, used to fish out in the bay for shrimps with a hand net. He would make his way to the shore regularly during the season, carrying his net over his shoulder and a hamper to hold his catch slung over his back. About a quarter of a mile from the water he would reach the channel, where he would push his net along the bottom to catch the shrimps. Returning home, he then boiled and picked them before going round the streets to sell them.

He often told how he had one dread, which was to be taken ill whilst out on the sands on his own. He therefore always left a lantern lit in the kitchen window when he went out shrimping. It could easily be seen by the neighbours, who made it their job to keep an eye open. If the light were still there at daybreak, they would know that something was wrong.

The inevitable occurred. The lamp was seen still alight one morning and so the neighbours could only think the worst had happened. A couple of local chaps who had knowledge of the sands volunteered to go out in search of him, but found nothing until the third day. They then went over the area they had searched for the last couple of days and there they found the body of the fisherman wrapped inside his net. He was found in the spot where for most of his life he had pushed his net in search of shrimps. It is said that the Bay never releases a body until the third day, by which time it will float to the surface.

Fishermen used to be away from home for long hours, going out on the ebb tide and returning on the flood. Weather could change quickly without warning and there were no radio forecasts to tell when a gale was expected. They had to depend on their own knowledge and a freak storm could catch them unawares, sometimes with disastrous results.

In 1911 a howling gale sprang up as two brothers and their cousin – all members of the Robinson family – set out from the Sandgate shore, Flookburgh, in their boat. Along with other village fishermen they were heading for the mussel grounds at Bardsea on the Ulverston side of the Bay. They worked hard, almost filling the boat with mussels, so that as they made for home it was very low in the water and ran aground. Before the tide could lift the boat, it was smashed to pieces and the three men drowned. The rest of the fishermen returned safely to Flookburgh as their boats were not so heavily laden.

This tragedy was related to me by a dear old lady who was born and bred in the village of Flookburgh and for whom I have always had the greatest respect. She said she remembered the night as if it happened yesterday. People were gathered around in small groups talking of the disaster, when Mrs Robinson, wife of one of the drowned men, came out of her cottage in Main Street and said, "What are they all talking about? You all look very sad."

Being deaf, she had some difficulty in making out what was being said. Then she heard her husband's name mentioned and something about a boat being lost. "Oh no. Don't say its my Ned," she exclaimed.

All the villagers were silent, until at last one of their number took her gently by the arm, led her towards her cottage and told her what had happened. My friend Ethel said the bodies of the two brothers were found washed up on the sand very early the next morning, but it was a month later before a dredger that was deepening the channel at Morecambe picked up the body of the cousin. He had left a wife and two small children.

In his sermon at the funeral the vicar remarked that these tragedies often struck more than once as in this case, where two of the victims were brothers and the third their cousin. It was a very sad day for the relatives and for the villagers.

Fatal Call of the Running Tide

Morecambe Bay, for all its beauty, is still a dangerous environment and a danger to the unwary. Fast running tides can cut you off from the safety of the shore, there is the dreaded fog and large areas of quicksands and mud that cannot be marked or mapped because of their frequent movements. At holiday resorts around the Bay and on the shoreline, notices are placed warning of the dangers but, occasionally, people do wander out onto the sands and accidents happen. Normally those living locally are more careful but sadly this does not always apply.

In July 1987 I had a telephone call from the Lancashire Constabulary at Morecambe telling me that two teenagers were missing, presumed drowned on the treacherous sands. What had started out as a long awaited seaside treat from a children's home ended in tragedy. A short while after arriving at a holiday caravan site the two excited young lads went out for a stroll and vanished in the fast incoming tide of the Bay. They had been told of the dangers of tidal currents, which have claimed many lives in the area out from Bolton-le-Sands, but they did not heed the warning.

When they failed to return that night a massive search operation got underway. Emergency services, including Arnside Inshore Rescue Team and mounted police, began a long and painstaking sweep of the coastline. At 8.45am on the Monday morning an RAF helicopter discovered the body of 16-year old Gary Thompson of Bilborough, Nottinghamshire. He was on the sands at Jenny Brown's Point, just south of Silverdale, some two miles up the Bay from where he had drowned.

A further extensive search in the area was carried out on the Monday and Tuesday, but no trace of 18-year old John Lindsay Thwaites of Beeston, Nottingham, could be found. Among the search and rescue teams were the distraught parents of the young lad and the police advised them to come over to Guide's Farm and have a chat with me about the terrible tragedy. When they arrived I was out in the Bay fishing and Olive was on her own so she invited them in. When I returned, quite late that night, I cleaned myself up a bit and we all sat round the fireside with a cup of tea.

At first I felt very uneasy explaining to them how this could have happened. Although they were upset they were able to control their emotions, but what they could not understand was how their son had been drowned because he was such a superb swimmer with many medals to his name. I explained about the particularly high tides that had come into the Bay with such force. Previously, the same area had been relatively safe, but with the River Kent changing its course to the Silverdale side it had now become dangerous with deep gullies and quicksands. These two poor young lads just did not stand a chance.

The parents did not want to leave the area until John's body had been found, so I suggested that they should stay over one more day. The police were in touch again at this stage asking for my advice on where to concentrate the search. With the tidal currents being known to me, I suggested that they now looked in one area only. This was the long seaward facing wall out into the Bay from Jenny Brown's Point, which acts as a barrier against the incoming tide and was the most likely place to find the body. The next day he was spotted from a helicopter alongside the wall, partly covered with sand. If he had not been found on that tide, he might never have been seen again as he would have been buried under the sands. I received a letter of appreciation from the Chief Inspector of Police, Len Parry, for my assistance given during the search and recovery of the two young men.

In August 1996 Terry Howlett, a 29-year old from Darlington, left home for a night out in Carnforth, a place he used to visit when on leave from the navy. After deciding to walk out on the beach at Cote Stones near Warton, he realised he was in trouble when crossing a gully and his feet were sinking. The more he struggled the deeper he went up to his waist. Eventually, he ceased sinking and the sand around him set like concrete. His shouts for help were not heard because of the wind and driving rain. How he survived the night is a miracle but the next morning a Mr Gardner fortunately heard his cries for help from his farm close to the shore. He called the police before seeking reinforcements. Fire, police and paramedics arrived, along with the Arnside Coastguards, but time was running short as the tide was well on its way in. By the time Terry Howlett was pulled clear the water was up to his neck and rising fast with some of the rescuers actually working below the surface. He was immediately airlifted by an RAF helicopter to the Royal Lancaster Infirmary suffering from hypothermia. Terry felt immensely grateful to the rescue teams who really did save his life - another ten minutes and he would have drowned.

A reconstruction of this incident was shown on the BBC TV '999' programme when the filming was done close to Morecambe Lodge Farm at Bolton-le-Sands. A stunt man was used, as they could not persuade Terry to repeat the performance! I was invited along as technical advisor for the making of the film, which was a quite different role for me but one I enjoyed to the full.

Search and Rescue

In 1977, John Duerdon of Arnside Coastguard asked if I would be interested in joining their Auxiliary Service reporting station. I readily agreed and was officially enrolled. I am still an Auxiliary Coastguard and have watched with great interest a recent development that is a huge asset in safety terms. Stuart Hamilton, secretary and treasurer of Bay Hovercraft Rescue, takes up the story:

"In 1996 the Coastguard Team of Arnside received an emergency call to attend a man who had been stuck in the quicksand out on the Bay for almost ten hours. He had walked out on a part of the sands not easily observed from the shore and had found himself stuck, and then sinking in a very wet and dangerous piece of quicksand. His cries for help had gone unheard for many hours, during which time he had sunk in up to his chest, and he was aware that the tide must soon be on its way in.

Arnside Coastguard is probably one of the most experienced mud and quicksand teams in the UK, but this rescue was to prove to be a race against time in which they, and their rescue equipment, had to travel a considerable distance from their base and the shoreline to attend to the casualty whose life was in imminent danger. Indeed, the tide was already running in before they were able to extricate him by the use of 'water-lances', which force water down the sides of the legs and, in this case, the body of the trapped person in order to loosen the sand and free that person. Not only was the man at grave risk, but throughout the rescue operation the coastguards themselves were struggling to ensure they too did not also become stuck.

Two of the Auxiliary Coastguards involved in this rescue, Gary Parsons and Adrian Swenson, decided that there must be more effective ways, not only to transport rescue equipment across the sands (where even the most robust four-wheel drive vehicle would become quickly stuck), but also transport a rescue crew to people who, if not trapped in quicksand, could be at risk of being caught by the fast flowing incoming tide. Arnside Coastguard has a rib-craft that is invaluable when the tide is in but, as with most large estuaries, for large parts of the time there is little or no water in Morecambe Bay except in the narrow channel formed by the River Kent. If you cannot use the rescue boat then basically you have to walk out to the casualty or person(s) in trouble.

Gary and Adrian agreed that a hovercraft could be the ideal solution to enable the rescue crew and equipment to be taken out across sand and water without fear of the craft becoming stuck. A hovercraft would also be quick and would not be affected should the tide be coming in or going out: it would simply 'float' from one surface to another. From several discussions about the logistics of using a hovercraft (which incidentally neither the Coastguard or RNLI had any official view or intention to utilise as rescue craft at that time), Gary Parsons bought himself an ex-formula one hovercraft to 'see how one performed' over all the hazardous and potentially lethal shifting sands. After many outings, on a huge learning curve to become proficient at 'flying' his craft and finding out how you can crash one too, Gary was now absolutely convinced that a search and rescue hovercraft based in the bay could and would prove to be a valuable life saving asset.

His logic was that if someone was stuck in or on the sands and more than a few metres from the shore (and some people do get themselves into trouble well away from easy access from the more popular parts of the shore) and the tide was due in, then time was to be of the essence for the rescue team. A hovercraft could both search, and provide assistance and rescue, very quickly and go where no other vehicle could go. It would also take rescuers and their equipment, and thereby save long and sometimes hazardous walks across the sands. For search purposes, vast areas and distances can be covered in a way that only a helicopter could, but a hovercraft would be much cheaper.

Now a single-seater ex-racing hovercraft does not meet the specification for search and rescue purposes. Gary and Adrian began to research what sorts of craft were available, what they cost and so forth. Through various connections, both in the Coastguard and mountain rescue teams, they were put in touch with a wealthy local benefactor who was noted for her immense generosity towards mountain rescue teams in the Lake District and to the RAF helicopter teams from Boulmer in Northumbria. Discussions followed. It turned out that the lady in question had experience of the perils of Morecambe Bay many years ago when her then young son had become trapped in quicksands. His rescue had been traumatic and she completely understood the proposal put to her by Gary and Adrian about the value of using a hovercraft on the Bay for search and rescue purposes.

As a result, a cheque was handed over to what had then become the beginnings of Bay Hovercraft Rescue, or BHR as the team refers to it. In June 2001, Bay Hovercraft Rescue took delivery of a brand new Osprey 5, Mark 2 hovercraft. But this is to jump ahead of some key events.

With a promise of substantial funds to purchase a craft and trailer on which to transport it, came the issue of where to base it. Using their knowledge of the Bay, Gary and Adrian began to look for a site from which to base the operations of the craft. Amside was a possibility as a suitable launch site, but there was nowhere immediately suitable to house the craft. Other potential sites were looked at. A discussion with Cedric Robinson was to prove to provide the answer. He advised Gary and Adrian that they should approach Tim Rogers, the manager of the Abbot Hall Hotel at Kents Bank, where there was a very large and only partly used garage (an old wartime fire station) which could be suitable. It was also only a hundred yards from the shore, which is accessed down a lane and across the railway line onto a perfect launching slipway. Cedric had already 'put a word in' by the time Gary and Adrian approached the hotel. The Abbot Hall Hotel is part of the Christian Guild Holiday Centres. Tim Rogers, the then manager, was only too pleased to offer 'garage space' to BHR and, from there on, BHR was in business.

In August 2001, following initial trials of the craft in various parts of the Bay and from a farm near Leven, where the River Kent outfalls into the Bay, BHR had its formal public launch at an event at Abbot Hall. The craft was officially named Lady Ada, after our benefactor Mrs H, by Lord Cavendish of Furness. The event, on a rather cold and wet day, was attended by members of Coastguard teams from all around the Bay and many members of the public from Grange. By this time BHR had increased its membership and this event brought more local volunteers on board. The official launch was one thing but BHR was not yet ready to be operational as an 'additional facility', that is to be a resource to be called upon by the Coastguard and other emergency services. The craft had several teething problems to be sorted out. Pilots had to be trained and various pieces of equipment, such as handheld VHF radios, were required. The major stumbling block, however, came down to insurance. Public Liability Insurance is an absolute necessity in this day and age. Finding an insurance company to provide cover seemed to be impossible. No one had ever set up a search and rescue operation using a hovercraft in the UK before. Underwriters did not want the

Hovercraft are now regarded as an invaluable part of the Morecambe Bay rescue service. Able to go almost anywhere on land or water, they can very quickly reach areas that a conventional craft or vehicle would find impossible.

business, or if they did they wanted many thousands of pounds for minimal cover.

Without insurance (and we had no problem covering it for theft and fire!), training pilots and crew was not possible in a public area. Arguably, there's less chance of running someone over in the middle of the Bay than there is of having an accident in a car in the middle of Grange, but BHR couldn't take the risk. It took several months of many phone calls and lengthy searches on the Internet before we made contact with a shipping insurer in Kent. If funding and Abbot Hall had been the first two 'miracles', then Everards was the third. Insurance was secured, not cheaply but at a reasonable cost for good cover.

Local support for BHR has been brilliant with funds and donations coming from a wide range of sources. In November 2001, BHR registered as a company and in February 2002 it gained status as a registered charity.

A great deal of time, effort and hard work has gone into forming BHR and getting it to a point whereby operational cover is available during evenings and weekends. Continuous cover is some way off, but tremendous progress has been made and we strive to improve and develop. BHR received its first call out from the Coastguard in late July 2002 and the craft was launched to attend an incident beyond the viaduct at Arnside. Once launched at Kents Bank, it literally takes eight minutes to cross the Bay (somewhat quicker than a crossing with Cedric on foot) and about twelve minutes to get under the viaduct. The incident, involving a sailing dinghy and a distraught owner, was dealt with swiftly and safely. The craft and its crew had to negotiate both tidal channels and dangerous areas of sands to carry out this rescue but it proved the point that a hovercraft was the only vehicle that could have done this.

Shortly after this BHR took ownership of two all-terrain vehicles called Argos. These vehicles are about ten feet long, four feet six inches wide, have eight-wheel drive, carry up to six people, and are semi-amphibious. Used widely on the Scottish shooting estates, and in Canada from where they originate, the Argos were seen as filling the final gap in additional safety provisions on the Bay. The Coastguard's rib-craft meets the requirements for rescues when the tide is in or running on a big tide. The hovercraft can cross the sands very quickly and virtually go anywhere on sand or water (as long as the latter is not excessively rough) in the Bay and can provide safety cover for the many cross-Bay walks that Cedric leads.

However, anyone familiar with the 'spartina problem' off the front of Grange and other parts of the Bay will understand that a hovercraft will have some difficulties flying over the rough spartina and the hidden channels that run through it. Quite simply, the craft loses too much air from its cushion, due to the rigidity of the grass, for it to fly effectively. The Argos were bought to ensure that no part of the Bay is not accessible to search and rescue teams. They have no problem in negotiating this rapidly expanding colonised shore area.

Such is their flexibility as rescue vehicles that they can cover the shore and grass areas whilst the hovercraft covers all the sands beyond. The Argos are available to local mountain and fell rescue teams to provide logistical support to their operations. They also climb up very steep hills!

Bay Hovercraft Rescue has come a very long way since Gary and Adrian first thought about using a hovercraft as a search and rescue vehicle. The resources of BHR have increased considerably and the team is developing its skills and knowledge. We have learned a great deal, both about flying a thing that has no brakes and feels like driving a car on ice, and about the Bay and how it constantly changes. We are all much more aware of what a perilous place it can be for the unwary.

It was celebrations all round at Morecambe when a £250,000 appeal to fund a permanent home for the station's hovercraft was surpassed and an amazing £315,000 was raised. The hovercraft Hurley Flyer is currently stored in temporary accommodation kindly loaned by Morecambe Yacht Club. This location has limited facilities and is situated some distance from the sea and possible launch sites. The crew has to collect the hovercraft on a transporter and then often have to negotiate heavy traffic prior to launch. On return from a callout the crew has to recover the hovercraft, then clean and carry out safety checks prior to moving and stowing the craft in the remote facilities. The new 'Home for the Hover', near Morecambe's Stone Jetty, will provide purpose-built accommodation with direct access to the main launch area, saving vital minutes.

Apart from the use of hovercraft, there has also been another major breakthrough. Gary Parsons, chairman and founding member of Bay Search and Rescue, explains:

"In 2005 I managed to pull off a deal with a military supplier in which we ended up owning a Hagglund Amphibious Tracked Personnel Carrier. This has proved to be the most versatile rescue vehicle ever used in the Bay. The Hagg – as it is affectionately known – beats the hovercraft hands down in all-round usefulness. It carries seventeen personnel, it travels across the quicksand fully loaded, it will climb up and down wherever it is pointed and it also swims – albeit slowly with an odd leak here and there!

The first rescue we did with the Hagg involved a ten-year old boy, who had been playing football with his mum and dad out on the sands at Park Wood caravan site near Holker Hall. The family Labradors had collided with him and fractured his femur clean in two. We were called by the police to assist the ambulance service as they could not reach him. It was not until we were called that we realised the tide was due. As it turned out the tide would not have reached him but, at the time, we could not take that chance. It took fifteen minutes to assemble, fifteen minutes to travel there and two minutes to drive out across the sands and bring the boy back to the waiting ambulance.

We have now moved from our first home at the Abbot Hall Hotel and are operational from our new station and visitor centre. This is close to South Lakeland Leisure Centre, a mile due south of Flookburgh along Mile Road. We are twenty-five yards from the shore and have an airfield right next to us. Two fixed wing planes are a named resource for long searches. I look upon our charity and our team as a leading force for Search and Rescue in the north of the country."

Towards a Tragedy

My father died in April 2006 at the wonderful age of 102 years. He fished the Bay from Flookburgh for most of his working life and was also born in the village. He had a remarkable memory and was a mine of information as he was always interested in what was going on and was kept up to date with all activities. When large areas of cockles were found off Aldingham, he said he had never known such an occurrence on the west side of the Bay in all his lifetime.

It was a really good thing for the local fishermen, but news spread rapidly and soon they no longer had the cockle grounds to themselves. There was an invasion of cockle gatherers, including Polish and Chinese immigrants, from the North East, Liverpool and North Wales, all taking to the sands of Morecambe Bay. The first raid of cocklers from afar was in 1988. They came in vans, cars, pickup vehicles, wagons, quad bikes and the like, and any form of transport in whatever condition was taken out onto the sands. Some of the workers even walked out to the cockle beds. The cocklers seemed well equipped with waterproofs and waders but their equipment consisted merely of buckets, rakes, netting and cockle bags.

The access from the shore at Aldingham is a relatively safe one, but very few if any of these newcomers would know about the tides in this area. Instead they would rely on keeping an eye on the local fishermen. They were not only fleecing the cockle beds but were turning the foreshore into a tip, leaving rubbish daily with no thought for the local inhabitants living nearby. It became an eyesore.

My good friend Mike Carter, who works for South Lakeland District Council, told me that one day he was surveying for rodents along the waste ground between the road and the shore at Aldingham. He found the remains of several small fires with cockleshells near each of them, as if people had been cooking them as you would bake potatoes on a campfire. A few days later in the same area he passed a piece of plastic sheeting with a pair of wellingtons sticking out at one end, so he gently tapped them with his boot and suddenly a head bounced up from the other end of the sheet. These cocklers must have been living rough and sleeping under the stars.

On another occasion a sensible resident called the emergency services, fearing numerous Orientals were being cut off by the tide. They were being escorted off when they saw the blue amber flashing lights on the shore and disappeared like scared rabbits.

With cockle beds being closed and even condemned in other areas and the demand creating a really lucrative business, new gangs were turning up to share in this bonanza. Anyone legally entitled to work in the United Kingdom can pick cockles in the Bay, but it was now a free for all and the local Flookburgh fishermen were getting worried about their future livelihood.

Access to the cockle beds from Flookburgh was at that time across land owned by Holker Estates. In order to limit the number of cocklers, permits now had to be obtained from the estate office. Humphrey Head became an easy option for these gangs to get themselves out onto the Bay, but soon this access point was also closed. This brought gangs to Kents Bank in large numbers.

I shall never forget talking to a holidaymaker on my way out to the fishing grounds. She was a very well spoken, elderly lady who told me that she had been coming to Kents Bank for her holidays for several years. She said that it was the nearest to heaven one could get whilst still living on this earth. That was quite true. A peaceful residential area for those with an urge to turn back the clock, it was a haven of peace and security in an increasingly naughty world.

Not for much longer as the cockle gangs began to turn up with vehicles parked from the railway station right the way up Kentsford Road. Cars, vans with trailers carrying quad bikes, pickups and the like were noisily coming and going at all hours with rubbish left behind day after day. Empty plastic bottles and old newspapers littered the roadside with no consideration at all for the residents. With the public toilets closed, the nearest bus shelter was used as a loo. Vehicles and tractors were regularly getting stuck on the shore and everywhere you looked was an eyesore.

Many organisations worked together in a bid to solve the problem, with public meetings being attended by the local police, representatives from Grange-over-Sands and South Lakeland District Councils, English Nature, North Western Sea Fisheries, Railtrack and Holker Estates. But it was the hard work and determination of the local community that definitely helped to swing the decision to close the access from Kents Bank station to the cockle beds. There was a great sigh of relief when this happened, although the shore was left looking like a battlefield. My own concern centred on whether this area would ever be the same again for me to lead walkers on the last stretch of the journey to the Kents Bank shore.

As time lapsed and cockles got harder to find, some of the gangs drifted away to the other side of the Bay. This still left the Polish workers who had accommodation at Kents Bank and were taken out to the cockle beds daily, according to the tides, and many Chinese cockle gatherers, whose transport seemed mainly to be on quad bikes. I have seen groups of Chinese walking back all of the seven miles from the cockle beds.

I always walk the sands prior to my busy season of walks and in April 2000 I had never seen a set of young cockles covering such a large area in all my working life. The sands were hissing with these young 'wheeat' as they are called at this early stage. From leaving Priest Skeer there was just one mass of young cockles in every direction as I made my way towards the River Kent near to Jenny Brown's Point.

When I arrived back at Guide's Farm I told Olive of my find, but I did say to her, "I doubt if they ever will be gathered as they are in a dangerous and difficult area." Access would have to be from Morecambe Lodge Farm, Bolton-le-Sands, via Priest Skeer and the notorious River Keer. The River Kent separated the Flookburgh fishermen from these beds but, as it takes a cockle two years to become sufficiently sizeable for gathering, there was no activity in the Morecambe area from the gangs of cocklers until November 2002.

A large trawler then moved close to the shore near Princess Crescent, Morecambe, causing outrage among local people. The North West and North Wales Sea Fisheries Committee had given permission for fishermen from the Dee estuary near Chester to come here and gather cockles from Morecambe Bay. The beds on the Dee were closed owing to contamination, the cockles being unfit for human consumption because of algal poisoning. About forty fishermen came at first, but within a week there were more than a hundred working the cockle beds. Gangs now arrived from Liverpool and North Wales, enticed by high prices and very rich pickings.

The local Morecambe fishermen, who had been looking towards making a good living all winter, feared that the cockle grounds would soon be depleted. Cockles were in great demand all over Europe and once the operation began an estimated fifty tons per day were being gathered, shipped by boat to Heysham Harbour and then on to processing plants in the United Kingdom and abroad.

I took a special interest in what was going on in the Bay, and on more than one occasion, had reason to be worried. Looking through my binoculars on a clear day I could see a group of people at least seven miles out from Kents Bank still working the cockle beds, with no transport anywhere to be seen and with the tide due. I was about to phone the coastguard services, when suddenly a person on a quad bike towing a trailer raced out from the shore at Kents Bank and across the wet sands. As I watched I could hardly see the bike for the spray, but at last he approached the Chinese cocklers and they ran towards him through the tidal water.

I was now really worried about safety on the sands for these people who had probably no idea at all of the tide and times in Morecambe Bay. I could see that something dreadful was waiting to happen.

Death of the Cockle Pickers

On the bitterly cold and windy night of February 5th, 2004, Olive and I returned home late from the University of Central Lancashire at Preston, to hear from our son Paul that twenty-two Chinese cockle pickers had been cut off by the fast rising tide in Morecambe Bay and drowned off Hest Bank. He had taken many phone calls on my behalf and been given numbers for me to ring back, as soon as possible. This I did, and spoke to someone at Liverpool Coastguard and to the police. Other calls were from journalists, but the only information I could give was from my own experiences and knowledge of the area where the tragedy had happened. Knowing the awesome power of the tides and the cruelty this Bay can deal out, I was left feeling numb.

All coastguard officers and teams around Morecambe Bay were called out that night to get out there and search. Liverpool Coastguard coordinated the whole operation. Police both locally and afar were also involved as were other services, ambulance crews and some of the local fishermen. Two Air Sea Rescue helicopters searched for survivors, and although it was dark, with a strong westerly wind, the lights from the shore that night could be seen clearly all around the Bay. From Guide's Farm we could hear the sound of a helicopter as it came up the Bay and could see a powerful beam of light scanning the surface of the water. There was also a flashing light from a moving vehicle, which we thought would be the hovercraft. One is always hopeful of finding survivors but, on such a night and with the water temperatures at this time of year being so low, there would have been very little chance.

Li Hua, a Chinese cockler, had only been in Liverpool for a few days and this was the first time out on the sands of Morecambe Bay. After picking a small bag of cockles, he felt it was too cold and too dark to continue, so he left the cockle beds, his colleagues and friends and found his way back to the shore alone. A short time later his mobile was called by one of his friends, who said that he was stuck in the sea.

Li Hua was a good swimmer and ran to try and rescue him. He swam across the first channel and was trying to swim the second when the waves and the tide became too strong for him to go any further. Desperately trying to save his drowning friend, he became stuck on a sandbank where he was seen by a helicopter and then rescued by lifeboat. His friend, who he called Brother Wen, sadly drowned. Tired rescue teams risked their own lives as they searched for survivors. All coastguard teams in Morecambe Bay, Walney and Millom received the Rescue Shield for their work that night.

Some three months after this terrible tragedy the Roman Catholic Bishop of Lancaster, the Right Reverend P. O'Donahoe, organised an Inter-Faith Memorial Service in the Cathedral Church of St. Peter. All the emergency services and rescue teams were represented and one member from most teams carried a candle to the altar.

The Catholic Archbishop of Liverpool, the Most Rev. P Kelly, gave the address and pointed to a painting he had brought of fishing boats moored at anchor. He said it reminded him of his hometown of Morecambe where, as a young boy, he would watch the trawlers all calm and serene on a nice day. But when he looked out, as he often did, he would watch them struggling against the wind to get out on the tide and back in again to a safe anchorage. It made him reflect on that cold winter's night in February. He went on to say that he had walked over the sands with a group

The Bay, looking calm and serene in this view from the old pier at Hest Bank. It seems difficult to believe that this was the setting for the needless death of twenty-two men on the cold and windy night of February 5th, 2004.

led by the Queen's Guide – Mr C. Robinson. M.B.E. He said it was a marvellous experience on such a lovely warm day in summer, but it must have been very different on that February weekend. It had brought back to him how the moods of the Bay keep changing.

Following the tragedy I received a phone call from the police at Preston Special Branch and C.I.D. The caller said, "You won't know me, Mr Robinson, but I already feel as if I know you. I crossed the Bay with you, on one of your walks when I was much younger and I have a certificate hung on the wall in my bedroom at home to prove it."

It was agreed that he would pay me a visit at Guide's Farm so that we could have a chat about the Bay and give him more insight and information about the cockle beds following that fateful night. He was a very nice chap and, as we settled down with a cup of tea, we got on to the question and

ROYAL NATIONAL
LIFEBOAT INSTITUTION

West Quay Road, Poole, Dorset, BH15 1HZ.

MORECAMBE LIFEBOAT STATION

[signature]

A report has been received from your Deputy Divisional Inspector concerning the services by the Morecambe inshore lifeboat and inshore rescue hovercraft on 5 and 6 February 2004.

Although there are some services that are distressing there are, fortunately for the Institution's crews, very few lifeboat services of the magnitude of that faced by Morecambe on 5/6 February 2004. An initial call to a vehicle in difficulty on the sands at low water, developed into a major SAR operation of nearly 20 hours, and ended, sadly in the crew recovering 11 bodies.

The leadership and dedication of your Lifeboat Operations Manager, Mr John Beaty, is being recognised separately. This letter is written in recognition of the contribution made by all the station's shore helpers and crew members.

I will start with those on shore. DLA Michael Guy, and shore helpers Adrian Sweeney, David Smith, Clive Rawles and Steve Hemmingway did all, and often more, than any operational crew can ask their supporting shore helpers to do. Helmsman Steve Wilson and crew members Keith Donaldson and Philip Smedley took over the D class and its searching for a while on the afternoon of 6 February.

Helmsman Michael Dixon with Carl Sadler and Paul Turner had originally launched D564 at 2124 on 5 February and saved one man from the sea at 2145. After the man was transferred to shore by the hovercraft they continued searching until 0418 on 6 February. The sea conditions were challenging for a D class and the transfer of the casualty to the hovercraft was particularly well handled.

This was the first major service involving an RNLI hovercraft. Under the command of Harry Roberts, and crewed by Andy Butler, Dave Berry and Michael Wood, the hovercraft was operating very close to its capabilities in view of the sea conditions. Sadly it fell to the hovercraft's crew to recover 11 bodies from the mud.

Despite the tragic circumstances, the actions of Morecambe lifeboat station have been inspirational. On behalf of the Council I would like to thank all of you for your teamwork and dedication during such a long, distressing and demanding service. Very well done, indeed!

Yours sincerely

[signature]

Morecambe Lifeboat Station received this certificate from the Royal National Lifeboat Institution in recognition of its work on February 5th and 6th, 2004. It praises its 'teamwork and dedication during such a long, distressing and demanding service'.

The Priest Skeer area of the Bay, off Bolton-le-Sands, where the only successful rescue took place on the tragic night of February 5th, 2004.

answer part, which went on for quite some time. All in all, he seemed to write about twelve pages from what I told him. He thanked us for our time, the information and our hospitality. This information, he said, would be read out in court to the judge and jury. At the time I thought that I would not hear from him again – but I did. It was alleged that the Chinese cocklers were the victims of exploitation by Snakeheads from Triad groups, who were accused of 'people trafficking'.

The cockling story would carry on through 2004 with the Lancashire police criminal investigation and multi-agency plans to police cockling, review safety standards and implement tougher licensing. As Olive and I were sat watching television one evening at 9.30pm, the telephone rang. On the other end of the line was someone from Australian Radio. He said that his name was John Kenneally and he was pleased to have been able to get through to me. He asked if I would agree to go out 'live' the following day on their Adelaide morning radio show. He said that over there they had heard so much about the tragedy of the cockle pickers, that it would be nice if I would talk about something else. So I agreed to speak on the pleasure the Bay gives to thousands of people who each year cross safely on the organised walks. It seemed so very easy to speak over the phone to an Australian radio station. His voice was as clear as a bell and my voice was heard live all that way from Morecambe Bay and Grange-over-Sands.

On September 20th, 2005, I was invited to attend Preston Crown Court to give a detailed account of the sands and tides in the area of Morecambe Bay where the Chinese cockle pickers had lost their lives. It was quite an ordeal for me, as I had never been in a court before and I felt quite nervous whilst standing in the witness box for about an hour. The following day the trial judge, Mr Justice Henriques, and the jurors went to see for themselves the place where the cockle pickers had drowned. They wrapped up well and donned their wellington boots, making the trip by hovercraft and familiarising themselves with the Bay. They were also taken to Priest Skeer, where the only successful rescue took place on that fateful night. The trial lasted six months and concluded with those directly responsible for the Chinese illegal immigrants and their sad deaths being found guilty.

In March 2006 I received a letter from the senior investigating officer into the Morecambe Bay tragedy, thanking me for my support and assistance and the manner in which I gave evidence. Mr Birrell said: "To assist the jury in understanding and following the volume of information, we turned to the latest technology to create a computer programme which allowed the prosecuting council to present and lead the jury through evidence about people, vehicles, maps, mobile phone records and everything that linked the defendants with the offences. This way of presenting the evidence saved more than a month of court time and was crucial in ensuring the defendants were convicted of the charges put to them. The Crown Prosecution Service called nearly one hundred and fifty witnesses including survivors and emergency service personnel who attended the tragedy. A variety of experts included:

- *Queen's Guide to Kent Sands, Morecambe Bay - a royally appointed expert who has knowledge of how the sands and channels shift on a daily basis.*

- *A scientist specialising in coastal and estuarine processes and the interaction of wind and tides.*

- *Several cockle pickers with many years experience in the industry, making them experts in their field.*

- *A forensic accountant who could interpret the Eden company's financial information which changed once they started to employ Chinese gangs.*

- *A handwriting expert who could suggest who had been responsible for organising false cockling permits."*

Mr Birrell added: "I would like to give my thanks to the many witnesses who have come forward to give evidence in court and contributed to this prosecution, especially those who had to relive the trauma of that tragic night."

A film 'Ghosts', based on the Morecambe Bay tragedy, has got its facts wrong and upset the local fishing community. It portrays the Chinese cocklers as victims of racism, forced to go and gather cockles in the dark because they were scared of intimidation by rival local fishermen. That claim has been strongly denied, as there was never any opposition from locals. 'Ghosts', written and directed by film maker Nick Broomfield, had a premiere screening at the Dukes' Theatre in Lancaster and at the Electric Cinema in Notting Hill, West London.

Part 5
Changing Times

Work and More Work

When we moved to Guide's Farm in October 1963 we found we had a lot to do to make ourselves comfortable. Everyone was willing to help and work day and night if necessary, as this was my busiest time on the sands.

Fishing was my livelihood, with shrimping in full sway. I kept my tractor and fishing gear on my parents' land in Flookburgh as there was no access onto the sands at Cart Lane or Kents Bank station owing to the River Kent then running close to the rocky shore. Having progressed from the horse and cart era into the tractor age, the long weary journeys in all weathers were now almost halved.

The magnificent location of Guide's Farm, seen from the back of the house, with the broad sweep of Morecambe Bay stretching away into the distance. (John Clegg)

Cedric and Olive, framed by the front doorway of Guide's Farm. (Peter Thompson)

Trawling for shrimps in the Bay is only the start, as most of the work with inshore fishermen begins when you arrive home. To make it easier for Olive I would lay the fire, sticks and coal to heat the boiler, and give her an idea of the time when Bill and I would return with our catch. This helped as she lit the fire in readiness and the shrimps could then be put straight into the boiler. They were later spread out on trays to cool, riddled and were ready for 'picking'.

Guide's Farm was always a busy but happy house. At weekends and during school holidays we would be full of children all sitting around a large table in the centre of the room picking shrimps. They were a good help and could earn a little money for themselves. It was quite common at Guide's Farm to see people sat round the living room table picking away until late at night. After everyone had gone home, Olive would set about to clean and wash down. We had oilcloth on the table and linoleum on the floors as coconut matting was a luxury.

If there was no shrimping and no cockles were to be found in the Bay, we were kept very busy making holly wreaths and crosses for Christmas, which my parents sold on Barrow-in-Furness outdoor market. We made hundreds of them and it was hard work, so much so that Olive's fingers became septic with the constant pressing and bending of the wires through the moss and holly. She never grumbled, although it did take them a while to heal properly.

There was very little time to prepare for Christmas but Olive always made the living room cosy and warm and it was a happy time for us. There was a lovely big open fire and a Christmas tree in the corner of the room. There were no lights - only two oil lamps that hung down from the large beams - but we had lots of decorations and so many Christmas cards.

It was usual when the family had gone up to bed on Christmas Eve for Olive to leave a glass of wine and a carrot on the hearth - the wine for Father Christmas and the carrot for his reindeer! The next morning there were large red socks hanging up at either side of the fireplace full of all sorts including oranges, apples, nuts and presents that Father Christmas had delivered down the chimney. Everyone was so happy that the wine had been drunk, the reindeer had eaten the carrot and Father Christmas had left the children lots of toys and gifts.

The winter seemed long and we were looking forward to the day when we could have electricity brought to the house. We had been using oil lamps and candles for almost six months - although it seemed much longer. After applying to the Electricity Board things soon got moving and in February 1964 the work was finished and the current was turned on. This changed all our lives, but none more so than that of Olive.

Christmas time at Guide's Farm, complete with a big open fire.

Cedric sawing logs to ensure an adequate supply of fuel for the winter.

When no cockles were to be found in the Bay we had long winter months without any money to be made. Things got desperate so I took a job along with a fishing pal of mine, Brian Shaw, at a factory in Barrow-in-Furness known as Listers, where we were each put in charge of a loom. The noise was terrible. Neither of us had clocked in for a job before in our lives - but here we were, desperate to have a go. It was so warm in the factory that we wore only what was essential, with no shirt and just a vest, trousers and carpet slippers. No one, except the supervisor, ever spoke a word to either of us. It was as if we had some sort of infectious disease! I stuck it out for only two weeks and was out of there like a shot. As bad as things were on the sands, this was not a job for me.

An opportunity arose to work on the site of the new Heysham Power station. A local character, George Broadhurst, had a contract with a firm digging trenches and laying electricity cables and he was looking for labourers. I joined his team of local lads and we used to pick George up at Cartmel in the early morning and arrive at Heysham just as it was getting light.

This was wintertime and nearly every morning we would grab our picks and shovels, jump into a trench with snow and ice still around and work like navvies. When the weather eventually broke down and the rains came, every worker except our gang would go under cover. After a while other men on the site approached George asking him if we were in the union. His reply was, 'The only union we will be joining is the Mothers' Union and you can go to hell!' Not long after it was decided that if we did not join we would be out of a job. We joined. However, when spring arrived I decided to give in my notice as it was time to start fishing again.

Farm Enterprise

There is very little payment from the Duchy for my services as Guide - £15 per year - but Guide's Farm is a smallholding with some ten acres of good land, so I wrote to the trustees and got permission to cultivate the part behind the house. As I already had a Ferguson tractor and the implements for ploughing and the like, we could now grow our own vegetables, catch flukes from the Bay, have fresh eggs from our own few hens that we had recently purchased and be almost self-sufficient. In summer we put a sign outside the garden gate reading 'Fresh Fish for Sale'. I always filleted the flukes and my, were they good, beating your expensive plaice every time!

The railway runs past the house on an embankment and the drivers of steam trains, both passenger and goods, would stop on the run towards Barrow, jump down from the train and come to the wall to shout out their orders. They asked either Olive or myself what was available, so we would have the fish wrapped ready for them on their return. These were very good orders as the drivers who came from Carnforth had not tasted fluke for years, so they were really glad of them and we at the farm were thankful for their custom.

We next had the idea of buying some young cattle from the farm sales as they would keep the grass down and could be sold on as two-year olds. Bill, our eldest son, was very keen so we went ahead and things went well at first, even though it was a case of trial and error. We bought a suckler cow, on advice from a local farmer, and bred a jolly good calf from it. The mother was tied in a stall with the cowband and the calf was allowed to run loose and suckle when it felt like it. Unfortunately, the calf got its head into a bin where we kept the barley to feed the mother, bloated itself and died. This was a lesson we learnt the hard way.

Calves were much smaller forty years ago and when purchased from farm sales were put in hessian sacks with just their heads sticking out. They were then brought home in the back of the van. It is different today with most continental breeds being much bigger at birth so there is just no way you would be able to transport them in this manner.

I purchased two wooden poultry houses, one of them on wheels, from Mike and Henry Garnett and put them halfway up the paddock. The idea was to rear turkeys, buying them at six weeks old and getting them ready in time to sell for Christmas. These were large turkey whites that grew to tremendous sizes. They were kept inside at first and when old enough they ran free range but were always fastened up at night on account of foxes. Bill and I were late back from the sands one night and when we went up to the paddock to lock up the turkeys we noticed that six were missing. As we walked through the meadow towards the big ash tree the six turkeys were perched quite high up, so we both thought they would be safe until the morning. Not so, as very early I walked through the meadow and found them with their heads off, killed by a fox.

Haytime at Guide's Farm, a smallholding with four hectares of good land and what must be one of the world's finest views from a meadow. Cedric and Olive became virtually self-sufficient through rearing their own stock, growing vegetables and catching fluke from the Bay. They even supplied orders to local railwaymen, who – unseen by authority would stop their trains outside the front door! (Gary Taylor)

Cedric's granddaughter Amy takes a turn on the tractor during haymaking at Guide's Farm. (Cedric Robinson)

I was so annoyed that I decided to lay in wait for it the next morning. Just before daylight my son Robert and I walked up the paddock and found a secluded spot near an old well, camouflaged with bushes all around us. It was a wet and very quiet, misty morning as we sat hidden with a shotgun. We did not have to wait long before the weirdest barking began. I had never heard a fox bark before, and this seemed so loud I thought everyone in Grange would be wakened.

The fox could be heard coming towards us and passed not too far away but it was not light enough to see it. We both sat there till daylight and then Robert had to be in Grange for work at 7.30am so we left our hideout and headed up the field. Suddenly, we saw Master Reynard heading back but well out of range. Perhaps this was just as well as neither of us had shot at anything before! He had been on his rounds and was probably looking for the turkeys he had killed the night before, but he was unlucky this time.

As people pass Guide's Farm they may see Charlie, our horse, whose stable is a barn attached to one side of the building, and many of them bring a carrot or two to feed him. He is a very friendly animal and he looks forward to his treats. If he's not inside, he will be in the fields and a whistle will usually bring him down. On the farm there are also at present four bullocks and a goat, who all wander freely through the pastures. We have lots of hens that supply us, and some of the neighbourhood, with free-range eggs – when they aren't being broody! There is always lots to do on the farm, and I'm fortunate that my son-in-law, Raymond, helps me to look after it as I have my work cut out with the ever increasing demand for the Bay walks.

Walkers passing Guide's Farm always look out for its docile animals.

Today there is just one goat but here four are waiting to be milked. (Fred Broomfield)

"Summat in That Water"

When fishing was poor and no money was to be made on the sands, my father found work on local farms, either thinning turnips, muck spreading, haytiming or draining the land. One day he was asked by Jimmy Edgar, who farmed Field Head at Flookburgh, if he would look at a wet area in the paddock in front of the house and check the land drains. Dad told me that as long as he could remember that field had always had a 'dub' - a waterlogged area with rushes growing around it. When he dug to find the old drains, the one in question was running at full bore all the time so he put it back just as it was and told Jimmy that it must be a natural spring.

Nothing more was thought about the spring until after dad had bought our horse from Harry Shaw, a fisherman in the village. She was a chestnut mare standing about sixteen hands high and had a very quiet nature. She was good on the sands and in the water shrimping but had a mild form of illness that the local veterinary surgeon could not recognise, so she was never treated.

Grazing land was difficult to obtain after the war, so we stabled the horse and scythed the grass verges every few days. This was hard work and inconvenient, but then we were lucky and were able to rent a small paddock that had been taken over by the War Ministry. After we had put the horse in this paddock, which was an extension of the dub field with the spring water, we noticed in a matter of weeks that she became more sprightly and was a different animal. There was very little grass for her to eat but an endless supply of water.

Years later, when we had moved into Guide's Farm and our daughter Jean had left school, we owned several ponies as she and all her friends were 'pony mad'. Among them was a lovely but aged gelding we called Flash and he was not doing too well. We always had plenty of help with the ponies from eager youngsters, boys as well as girls. Gary Lynott used to come along from Flookburgh and now and again went out onto the sands with me to fish the fluke nets. Gary mentioned to his dad, Philip, that one of our ponies was not doing as well as it should have been, so Phil suggested that I should take it over to his place and put it in his paddock to see how it fared. It was the paddock with the dub in it - and the change was amazing.

I went along with dad about a fortnight later and we were leaning over the gate looking at our pony, when Phil spotted us and came down for a chat. The pony had had its head down for quite some time in the same spot and dad wondered what was up. We opened the gate and all three of us went over towards Flash. As it lifted its head, water dribbled from its mouth. Then all of a sudden it shot off round the paddock at full gallop, like a two-year old. Dad said, "Well I nivver, there must be summat in that watter that's done him some good."

Phil was so pleased to see such a change in Flash in so short a time. He later bought two ponies himself and stabled them because of their poor condition. Both of them had got strangles, a terrible illness that meant their throats had swelled and they had a nasal discharge. Spring came along and Phil took a chance by turning them out to grass in the paddock with the dub. There was very little for them to eat but after just a few days there was a remarkable improvement. Many years later Phil decided that he would like to know more about the spring on his land, so he went along to see my father. Dad has a remarkable memory and was able to show him the exact spot where the drain carrying the water could be found. Phil dug down, bricked round the spring and put in a manhole nearby. He kindly allowed me - and I believe dozens of other people - to take the water home and try it for ourselves.

Some years ago Phil, David Jones and Ian Needham gathered around the spring and decided to do something about it. A pump was installed and one of the most up-to-date bottling plants in the country built, so that the wonderful Lakeland Willow Spring Water could now be appreciated nationwide.

When I told dad about this, he said jokingly, "Aye, an' 'ad it nut bin for me, they wud nivver 'ad fund it, so I should have a share in it, shouldn't I?" "No" he added, "I wish 'em well and the best of luck with it. If tha sis 'im, tell 'im waint ta."

I certainly did and, at a later date, Phil gave me a tour of the new factory and bottling plant - and plenty of bottled water to keep us going for some while.

Lakeland Willow Water is under new management, having recently been bought by Cumbrian entrepreneur Brian Scowcroft. This unique water is being put forward for scientific trials following countless unsolicited testimonials from people – including celebrity food writer Clarissa Dickson-Wright. They all claim that skin and muscular skeletal conditions can be greatly eased by drinking the famous Willow Water.

Morecambe Bay Task Group

Lancaster District Council recently became concerned about the apparently growing problem of abandoned vehicles in Morecambe Bay. The main concern was the environmental impact from pollution created by these vehicles as they sank into the sands. The Council decided to set up a Task Group, on which I was asked to serve, and it began by visiting the affected area. However, the Group was advised that abandoned vehicles were now judged to be a historic problem and that new regulations would stop this happening in the future.

Remains of a motor vehicle on Flookburgh sands. Issues centred on the dumping of vehicles led to the recent establishment of a Morecambe Bay Task Group.

The Group, therefore, refocused its work to examine plastic pollution and its impact on the Bay. We live in a plastic convenience culture; virtually every human being on this planet uses plastic materials directly and indirectly every single day. Every year we eat and drink from some thirty-four billion newly manufactured bottles and containers. We patronise fast food restaurants and buy products that consume another fourteen billion pound of plastic. In total, our societies produce an estimated sixty billion tons of plastic material every year.

Each of us on average uses one hundred and ninety pounds of plastic annually – bottled water, fast food packaging, furniture, syringes, computers, computer diskettes, packing materials, garbage bags, and so much more. When you consider that this plastic does not biodegrade and remains in our ecosystems permanently, we are looking at an incredibly high volume of accumulated plastic trash that has built up since the mid-twentieth century.

Members really had their eyes opened to the impact such pollution has on marine life and the environment as well as the issues surrounding marine litter. Evidence was gathered from prominent scientists, Dr Richard Thompson, from the University of Plymouth, and Dr Jan van Franeker, from KIMO (Kommunenes Internasjonale Mijorganisasjon), which oversee the Save the North Sea project.

Dr Thompson's work had revealed the alarming amount of plastic fragments found in the sand on our beaches. Sand from different locations around the United Kingdom was analysed and micro plastics were found. This research was carried out down to the size of the width of a human hair and it is clear that still smaller particles exist in our sand. With most plastics being non-biodegradable, these micro plastics are becoming more and more microscopic and are being ingested by plankton and other filter feeders in all of the world's oceans. These are, in turn, being eaten by small fish, which are then consumed by larger fish. Marine mammals such as seals, whales and turtles eat these fish and end up with toxins accumulating in their bodies. This must beg the question of whether the fish we eat have ingested plastic particles and, therefore, plastic is entering our food chain. Unfortunately, no research has yet been undertaken on this point.

The research that has been carried out by Dr Jan van Raneker again unearthed startling realities of the impact that plastic pollution was having on the environment. Dr Franeker's work concluded that almost every seabird in the world has waste plastic inside its stomach. The stomachs of fulmars in the North Sea, storm petrels in the Antarctic and albatrosses in Hawaii have all been found to contain plastic discarded by consumers or industry. Some birds have eaten hundreds of plastic fragments and many have died as a result.

The Task Group learnt that leatherback turtles now live in Morecambe Bay and that plastic bags and balloons posed a great threat to these beautiful creatures as they mistook them for jellyfish and consumed them, causing death by asphyxiation or starvation. It was recognised that Lancaster Council, a small local authority, could really do little on its own to tackle this global problem. It therefore needed to seek support from other councils around the country to gain a voice that would be heard by the Government. The Group has made a number of recommendations, including opposing balloon releases in the district, encouraging the Government to introduce a tax on plastic carrier bags and to raise the target for plastic recycling, persuading cotton wool bud manufacturers to use biodegradable materials for the sticks, and supporting the 'Fishing for Litter' campaign.

Where does all the plastic go? There are only three places it can go – our earth, our air and our oceans. All the plastic that has ever been produced has been buried in landfills, incinerated or dumped into lakes, rivers and oceans. When incinerated, the plastics disperse non-biodegradable pollutants, much of which inevitably find their way into marine ecosystems as microscopic particles. Some 70% of marine rubbish sinks to the bottom, 15% floats on the surface and 15% is washed up onto the coasts. The Government recently published the national packaging recycling and recovery targets for 2006 and beyond. These require only 23% of plastic waste to be recovered by 2006, rising to 25.5% by 2010. This is compared to 68.5% for paper and 74.5% for glass in 2010.

Shifting Sands

Morecambe Bay is still an amazing place. Anyone who ventures out onto the apparently endless expanses of sand cannot help but be impressed and even overwhelmed by the vastness of the surroundings. When the tide is in the Bay can be deceptively calm but, in reality, it is an extremely dynamic place. Its broad funnel-like shape and shallow depth affect the tidal ebb and flow, creating strong currents. Tidal bores can roar over the sands at nine knots – the fisherman's term is 'as fast as a galloping horse'. These powerful tides move tons of sand, building up banks, gouging deep and muddy channels and scraping out 'melgraves', deep and dangerous holes that fill with quicksand and change daily.

Rivers carrying freshwater draining off the Lakeland and Lancashire fells pour into the Bay and carve channels into the sandflats. The River Kent, one of the fastest flowing in England, changes its course continuously. It has repeatedly swung from one side of the Bay to the other following great storms. These changes in the Kent channel have great impact on the shores of Arnside, Silverdale and Grange-over-Sands. Wide areas of salt marsh develop when it moves away from the coast, but when it veers back again the salt marsh is washed away.

A strong wind coinciding with a high tide can play havoc, hurling great waves, smashing embankments and breakwaters, and causing the sea to flood the low lying parts of the land. Yet at low tide these miles of quick and living sands are left bare for all to see. The three main rivers, Keer, Kent and Leven along with their associated dykes and gullies, wander out into the Bay and form new channels for themselves every tide.

Wherever the river runs is always the lowest part of the Bay with a strong ebb and flow of the tides. Large areas of sand are taken away each tide from dykes and gullies, which are soon unrecognisable and impossible to cross. The old cockle road across the Flookburgh marsh from West Plain Farm, which gave access to the fishing grounds for the fishermen, past and present including myself, is now a no-go area. It has been eaten away and eroded to such an extent by the River Leven that both the marsh and the road have come to an abrupt end.

My father once told me that the Flookburgh sea embankment was originally built in the late 1700s and ran from Humphrey Head to Cowpren Point. The reclaimed marsh or lowland was eventually farmed and a barn was built. The farmers grew tremendous crops on this sandy land, but in the 1800s the River Leven took a dramatic change of course and cut out from the Ulverston side of the Bay, running eastwards towards the Flookburgh embankment. It broke through the defences, leaving gaping holes and flooding the lowland at East Plain Farm with seawater. Eventually, a second length of embankment was built up to West Plain Farm as you see it today. In

Huge boulders of limestone being put in place as an emergency measure to protect the Flookburgh area from tidal flooding.

2004 the same River Leven was seen to be taking a similar course as in the 1800s.

I remember my father also telling me that the original sea embankments out from Flookburgh were built up from seashore sand and then turfed. Although sheep were allowed to graze the marshes and the embankments, it was up to the farm tenants to cut hawthorn bushes from the hedgerows and lay these along the embankments at intervals to prevent the sheep from making a permanent track, which would then have been a weak spot against the onslaught of the high tides. A gamekeeper from the Holker Estate would walk the embankment regularly to make sure that rabbits didn't burrow. There were lots of rabbits on the farmland in those earlier years, so they had to be kept at bay.

Overlapping and breaching of embankments occurred due to storms as recently as 1967, 1971, 1977, 1983, 1989 and 1990. The embankments were improved and raised in 1992 to provide a wider crest and improve the levels of protection. More recently, emergency measures have been taken by Environment Agency workers, who have put around 150,000 tonnes of limestone in the Flookburgh area to protect a caravan park and several properties from tidal flooding. The stones are reinforcing the turf covered sand embankment as the tidal channels were starting to get closer. Work had, therefore, to be done to prevent the tidal waters from undermining the base and to

The two figures on the skyline emphasise the scale of the sea defence works at Flookburgh.

defend any vulnerable points.

November 1977 was memorable for the residents of Grange-over-Sands and Arnside as high winds and tides gave our coastline its worst battering in years. Sea walls were wrecked, roads swamped, train services disrupted, power supplies cut and telephones put out of action. Boats were reduced to matchwood. The storm raged from the Friday, over the weekend and into the following week.

Grange's open air swimming pool, which was threatened with closure at the time, was badly hit. Thousands of pounds worth of damage was caused to the old pool and the promenade. Seats were twisted beyond recognition with slabs of concrete and boulders being hurled through the air and railings smashed. The bowling green and tennis courts were strewn with rocks and long stretches of the promenade walling were demolished. Train passengers had to be transported by bus, whilst workmen repaired the line near Holme Island. All along the coast of Morecambe Bay there were reports of serious damage. Our shed was uprooted, blown clear over the line and onto the shore where it was smashed to pieces. Luckily it did not come to rest on the railway line.

At Arnside, eleven boats were badly damaged, and two hundred feet of sea wall was reduced to rubble. John Duerden, the auxiliary coastguard, was called out as many houses in the village were flooded, but the key thing he was able to do was to make sure no trains came across the viaduct. The waves had thrown lots of debris onto the line and if a train had tried to cross it would have been catastrophic. John also made a tour of the village with the police to rescue people trapped in their cars on the main road. Boys from Earnseat School helped to clean up the village after the storm. Apart from the sea wall damage, the narrow coastal road running from Ashmeadow to the old boathouse, the most popular walk in Arnside, was almost completely wrecked.

At Silverdale, water engulfed the road between Slackwood Farm and the railway crossing. A taxi was submerged and washed over a hedge, but the driver managed to swim to safety. Many sheep were drowned and one resident of Silverdale said the scenes were reminiscent of the big floods in 1905.

In 1980 a dramatic change in the courses of the Kent and Keer altered the whole area of the Bay on this eastern side and out from Grange-over-Sands and Kents Bank, something which had never been seen within the memory of any living person. We have had to live with it, and the ever-increasing spartina grass that is now so well established not only here but all around our shores in Morecambe Bay.

The question often asked is whether the Kent will ever come back over this side of the Bay and get rid of the grass. You can never say never – the river will return sometime. High tides, heavy rainfall and gales will play a great part in shaping these dramatic changes, but one cannot always predict when they will occur.

I read an account of an extraordinary high tide on December 27th, 1857, which exceeded by twelve feet anything ever recorded before or since. Then there was the great gale of February 27th, 1903, when in the early morning hours the down mail train was blown over as it was crossing the Leven viaduct, fortunately without loss of life. When you read these accounts – and there have been many more recent instances – it is frightening to think what could happen in the not too distant future with rising sea levels. This is an important issue not only for us but for the next generation and one not to be taken too lightly.

Cedric and Olive with the Bernard Gooch Award, received in 1998 as 'Cumbria Personality of the Year for services to tourism.

Looking Ahead

Our continually increasing demand for water has in the past been met by bigger and bigger reservoirs, ousting communities and flooding vast areas of productive land, but the time may come when there are no more suitable valleys. What then is the alternative?

One possibility is barrages. In 1967 I was deeply involved with a survey, which I described in my book 'Sand Pilot of Morecambe Bay'. Experts in engineering, water supply, biology, economics, transport and many other fields made a detailed examination in a government sponsored £500,000 feasibility study, which took more than two years to complete.

The survey of the Bay wasn't easy and the weather was no help. Thirty-five boreholes were sunk from six drilling rigs, but they soon ran into trouble. Huge rollers on each corner, on which the rigs were mounted, proved unsuitable and special semi-permanent bases had to be built with scaffolding. Despite rain and storms, the drilling went down to three hundred feet.

In 1972, after five years of study, the Water Resources Board concluded that Morecambe Bay could be used for freshwater storage. Several different schemes were outlined. A full barrage twelve miles long, reaching from Hest Bank to Baycliff near Aldingham and carrying a dual carriageway road above it, would cost an estimated sixty nine to seventy three million pounds. A major disadvantage of this plan would be the probable extent of silting on the seaward side, putting at risk major ports such as Heysham Harbour, Fleetwood and Barrow. In fact, no recommendation was made as to whether or not the Bay should be developed and since then the project appears to have been shelved because of lack of funds. So, all that is now in the past but not forgotten and sometime in the future a barrage could become a reality.

I have recently read of plans to build a bridge across the Bay connecting Barrow and Heysham. The state of the art structure with wind turbines above it and hydro turbines below is the brainchild of Kendal based businessman David Brockbank. He claims that completion of the link would open the whole of the west coast of Cumbria to people from the area and further afield, just as George Stephenson did in 1836 when he proposed to take the railway straight across the Bay.

If a barrage were ever built, the livelihood of an extremely hardy, modest and very knowledgeable race of men and women would largely disappear. My job as Queen's Guide to the Sands would obviously become obsolete and all charities would loose out on their guided walks, which over the years have raised millions of pounds towards their funding.

I would have to reflect on my lifetime on Morecambe Bay. Fishing my nets at sunrise in the silent flatness of this huge Bay and watching the birdlife as the tides race towards the shore. The never to be forgotten sound of large groups of walkers, with dogs, all entering the River Kent at the same time, with everyone enjoying themselves. The wettings out there in the thunderstorms. The delight of just being out there and giving pleasure to so many people over the years, both young and old. Being filmed with celebrities, and there has been many over the years.

The most beautiful and amazing views and the sunrise and sunsets are a tonic to the system. One never gets tired of looking out across the Bay with its ever changing light. Nothing could ever compensate me for my memories of the past. If the Morecambe Bay barrage or bridge were to be built in my lifetime, I should miss something that has been part of me all my life. My constant challenge with quicksands, fast rising tides, swirling currents, deep tidal channels and the most stunning but notorious landscape. My second home – the sands of Morecambe Bay.

'One never gets tired of looking out across the Bay with its ever changing light.'

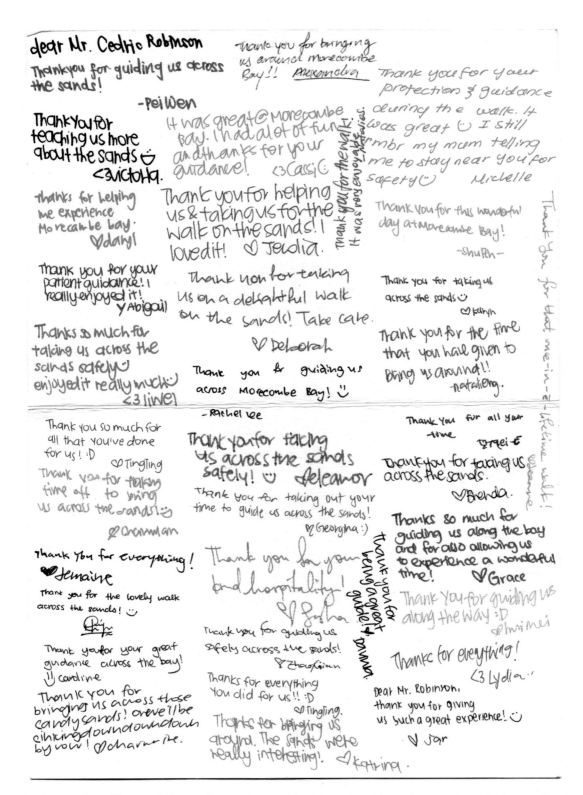

dear Mr. Cedric Robinson
Thankyou for guiding us across the sands!
-pei Wen

Thank you for bringing us around morecombe Bay!! Alexandra

Thank you for your protection & guidance during the walk. It was great :) I still rmbr my mum telling me to stay near you for safety :) Michelle

Thankyou for teaching us more about the sands :) <3victoria.

It was great @ Morecombe Bay. I had a lot of fun and thanks for your guidance! <3 Cassie

thank you for the walk! It was very enjoyable materials.

thanks for helping me experience Morecambe bay. ♥daryl

Thank you for helping us & taking us for the walk on the sands! I loved it! ♥ Jeudia.

Thank you for this wonderful day at morecombe Bay! -ShuFen-

thank you for your patient guidance! I really enjoyed it! ♥Abigail

Thank you for taking us on a delightful walk on the sands! Take care. ♥ Deborah

Thank you for taking us across the sands :) ♥kalyn

Thanks so much for taking us across the sands safely:) enjoyed it really much :) <3 liivei

Thank you for guiding us across Morecombe Bay! :)
-Rachel lee

Thank you for the time that you have given to bring us around!! -nataliemg.

Thank you so much for all that you've done for us! :D ♥Tingling

Thank you for taking us across the sands safely! :) ♥eleanor

Thank You for all your time ♥Mei E

Thank you for your kind hospitality! ♥Esther

Thank you for taking us across the sands. ♥Brenda.

Thank you for being a great guide! ♥Dawn

Thank you for taking time off to bring us across the sands! :) ♥Chenminan

Thank you for taking out your time to guide us across the sands! ♥Georgina :)

Thanks so much for guiding us along the bay and for also allowing us to experience a wonderful time! ♥Grace

Thank you for everything! ♥Jermaine

Thank you for the lovely walk across the sands! :)

Thank you for guiding us safely across the sands! ♥Zhaoxian

Thank you for guiding us along the way :D ♥wnmei

Thank you for your great guidance across the bay! :) caroline

Thanks for everything you did for us!! :D ♥Tingling.

Thanks for everything! <3 Lydia..

Thank you for bringing us across these sandy sands! or we'll be sinking down down down by now! ♥charmaine.

Thanks for bringing us around. The sands were really interesting! ♥katrina.

Dear Mr. Robinson, thank you for giving us such a great experience! :) ♥ jan

Cedric receives 'fan mail' from all over the world. This colourful card came from thirty pupils at Singapore Chinese Girls' School after he had taken them across the Bay in May 2007.

Subscribers

Brenda Allott	Zoe Brame	Joan A Cutts
Mrs J Almond	Mrs S E L Brayshaw	Patricia M Daniel
Jessie Anderson	Wayne Brennand	Mr Harvey William Davidson
Dave Antrobus	John Briggs	Alan R Dent
John & Janet Appleyard	In Memory of Adrian P Brodrick	Jenni Dickinson
Lydia Arnold	Richard John Bromley	S R Dobson
Naomi Arnold	J S Brook	Roy Aird Donaldson
Roger & Fran Arnold	Mr & Mrs S Brooksbank	Jane Douglas
Paul L Arro	Jean Broughton	M Downes
William K Asquith	Patricia Lillian Brown	Peter Draper
Alec Atkinson	Joan Wells Brown	Maria Duda
Lucy Atkinson	Sue Bryan	Susan Dugdale
David Paul Bailie	Ian Budgen	Mr Robert Dutton
John K Bailie	The Burgess Family	Katherine Duxbury
Kenneth Bailie	Pauline M Burgon	Heather Duxbury
Bob Baines	Miss J M Burrows	George R Eaton
Mary Baird	Neil Burtwistle	Frank Edgeworth
J Ballantyne	David Buxton	J M Edwards
John & Mary Barber	Louise Byass	Olga Batty Edwards
Edna and Raymond Barnard	Dennis Cairns	J G Eldon
Lorna Barnes	Will Calderbank	John Michael Ellis
Betty Barratt	Mike & Terry Carter	R M Estevez-Baker
David Barrell	Margaret Chapman	Derek Evans
Jean Barrett	Kathryn Clark	Ken Fairclough
Christine & LarryBennett	C L Clarkson	Robert Farquharson
Bryan Berry	Melanie Close	Malcolm Faulkner
Elisabeth Bertenshaw	Kevin Cochrane	Alan Flattley
S Hugh Binns	Ken Coulthard(Laversdale)	Mary Forrest
Mr George Binstead	Richard & Rosemary Crabtree	Audrey Foster
Corey and Rhys Birkett	Joan Craven	Miss Joan Frost
Ken Booth	Keith Cregan	David Gall
M H Bostwick	A R Crossland	Prof A S Garden
John Richard Bradley	Mr & Mrs W Crossley	Colin Gardner
W J Bradshaw	Betty Crowther	Mrs Jean Gadsden
Anne Braithwaite	Andy Curtis	Barbara Gibson

John H Gibson M.B.E

Mr Jack Gomersall

C E Granger

Mrs J M Greaves

In memory of Alan Green
(1927-2007)

Jean & Raymond Hadwin

The Haigh Family

Barbara Hall

Mrs J Hall

Scott R Hall

Hazel Harcourt

Nigel G Harding

Malcolm Harpin

Patrick Hart

Simon Hart

Keith Hartley

Ann Hastings

Daniel B Heath

John Hermansen

Tony & Judith Higgs

Richard F Hill

Geoffrey Hirst

Jamie Hirst

Norman Hitchen

Kevin Hobbs

Mrs Margaret A Hobson

Mary Holden

John & Mary Holland

Mark Nicholas Holliday

Timothy C D Hollis

Val Holmes

Dorothy Holt

Robert Hopkins

James Hornby

Mrs Maureen Horner

Brian & Norah Hosker

Philip Hughes

Mrs M Hullah

Alison J Hunt

Dorothy Hunt

Stanley Hutchinson

Margaret Illingworth

Edward B Ingham

Kenneth Ingham

Mary Irving

Mr & Mrs S G Ives

A I Jackson

David James

Malcolm G James

Ann & Sean Jamesom

Ann & Sean Jameson

Eric Jarvis

Linda Jenkinson

Judith Johnson

Steve Johnson

Ann Jones

J A Jones

Rosemary Jones

A & M Jowett

Jane & Barry Keelan

Guy Kilgallen

Andy Kilmartin

Michael S Kirk

John & Christine Kirkman

Sheila Knox

Michael Kyle

Frank Large

Judith Lawson

Margaret Lawson

John Laydon

Mrs J P Leach

Eileen Leak

Marlene Lee

Liz Lee

Richard Lees-Jones

Kevin & Amanda Lonergan
& Family

Roger Long

Stewart Longworth

Mrs Mary Lynn

Jean Makinson

J E Mallinson

John Mark

Elaine Marks-Parker

Carole J Marshall

Mr Stephen A Mashiter

Tom Mason

Jane McInerney

John Michael McNicholas

Kenneth Mills

Trevor S Mitchell

Ann Moore

Barbara & Trevor Moore
(Grange-over-Sands)

Constance M Morley

Alison Morse

Janice Moss

F J Mould

Alan Muckalt

Dorothy Murray

Andy Mortimer & Heather Naylor

Bill Nelson

Alan & Pamela Newton

Bill & Jacqui Nickson

Paul & Danielle Nickson

Robert & Tracey Nickson

Joan North-Coates

A C Nunn

S E O'Donnell

Steven Ogden

Richard Ogden

Mike & Penny Old

Trevor & Diane Park

Jean Parker

Melvyn Parker

Malcolm Pearce